DATE DUE

DEMCO 38-296

After
Authoritarianism

Recent Titles in
Contributions in Political Science

Curbing Unethical Behavior in Government
Joseph Zimmerman

How to Think About Social Problems: American Pragmatism and
the Idea of Planning
Hilda Blanco

The Origins of the Twelfth Amendment: The Electoral College in
the Early Republic, 1787–1804
Tadahisa Kuroda

Environmental Policies in the Third World: A Comparative Analysis
O. P. Dwivedi and Dhirendra K. Vajpevi, editors

Social Justice in the Ancient World
K. D. Irani and Morris Silver, editors

Securing the Covenant: United States–Israel Relations After the
Cold War
Bernard Reich

Why the Cold War Ended: A Range of Interpretations
Ralph Summy and Michael E. Salla, editors

Presidential Leadership and Civil Rights Policy
James W. Riddlesperger, Jr., and Donald W. Jackson, editors

The Eagle and the Peacock: U.S. Foreign Policy Toward India
Since Independence
M. Srinivas Chary

Japan's Role in the Post-Cold War World
Richard D. Leitch, Jr., Akira Kato, and Martin E. Weinstein

Botswana's Search for Autonomy in Southern Africa
Richard Dale

Contested Terrain: Power, Politics, and Participation in Suburbia
Marc L. Silver and Martin Melkonian, editors

12

AFTER AUTHORITARIANISM

Democracy or Disorder?

Edited by DANIEL N. NELSON

Contributions in Political Science, Number 360

GREENWOOD PRESS
Westport, Connecticut • London

Library of Congress Cataloging-in-Publication Data

After authoritarianism : democracy or disorder? / edited by Daniel N.
   Nelson.
           p.   cm. — (Contributions in political science, ISSN 0147–1066
   ; no. 360)
       Includes bibliographical references and index.
       ISBN 0–313–29393–7 (alk. paper)
       1. Democracy—History—20th century.   2. Authoritarianism—
   History—20th century.   3. National security—History—20th
   century.   I. Nelson, Daniel N.   II. Series.
   JC421.A36   1995
   909.82′9—dc20   95–5267

British Library Cataloguing in Publication Data is available.

A paperback edition of *After Authoritarianism* is available from Praeger
Publishers, an imprint of Greenwood Publishing Group, Inc. (ISBN
0–275–95330–0).

Library of Congress Catalog Card Number: 95–5267
ISBN: 0–313–29393–7
ISSN: 0147–1066

First published in 1995

Greenwood Press, 88 Post Road West, Westport, CT 06881
An imprint of Greenwood Publishing Group, Inc.

Printed in the United States of America

⊗™

The paper used in this book complies with the
Permanent Paper Standard issued by the National
Information Standards Organization (Z39.48–1984).

10 9 8 7 6 5 4 3 2 1

Contents

Introduction:
After Authoritarianism

DANIEL N. NELSON

Authoritarianisms come in many varieties. Armies, parties, oligarchies, corporatist business elites—all can be the locus of those who inaugurate and maintain authoritarian rule. But, they all share indelible markings that denote an elite's domination of society through state control.[1] Political structures are used to create authoritarianism, and enhancing their power is the *raison d'être* for authoritarian rule—power for the sake of power.

Twentieth-century authoritarianism has appeared, in some cases, immutable. The penetration of social, economic, military, and other structures by a ruling elite has thwarted many reformers who have sought, with great courage, to generate systemic change. Tragic consequences, such as the deaths at Tiananmen Square in June 1989, are recounted in this volume and imply the futility of opposing a well-entrenched authoritarian system.

Yet, by the late 1980s, a series of events—particularly among the communist systems of East Central, Southeastern, and Soviet Europe, but also including Nicaragua, other Latin American cases, and the Philippines' ouster of Marcos—led some observers to refer to a "globalization of democracy."[2] As the number of states ruled by one party, army juntas, corporatist cliques, and other permutations decreased, a "third wave" of democratization was declared.[3]

Whether or not these assessments are accurate, however, depends on answers to basic questions, for example, "What conditions make democracy possible and what conditions make it thrive?"[4] In the aftermath of authoritarianism, can the fear of and real potential for disorder be mitigated? Indeed, the sometimes delicate balance between democracy and disorder once decades of state control have been lifted is a matter of great urgency as we approach the end of the millennium.

At the Graduate Programs in International Studies, faculty and students began to address such fundamental questions in their research and seminars. Seeking a mechanism by which to focus interest in the subject of postauthoritarian transitions and a platform to stimulate additional research on comparative and transnational aspects of democratization, we planned and implemented a major conference in the spring of 1993. Integral to this conference, as distinct from many other efforts to grasp the seismic shifts under way in the late 1980s and early 1990s, were two important focal points—on *praxis* and on *security* as factors underlying possibilities for democratic development.

Framed by the theoretical insights of Yale political scientist Robert A. Dahl, the conference and this resulting volume then turn, in Part I, to the views of those who have themselves been agents of change—in the case of Raúl Alfonsín, leading Argentina's postauthoritarian transitions as his country's president, and in the cases of Liu Binyan and Floribert Chebeya, having been known as prominent opponents of Chinese and Zaïrean dictatorial rule. Part II's focus on the prognosis for ties between democracy and security has global applicability, although most of the examples are European. GPIS faculty Simon Serfaty and Regina Karp join Charles William Maynes (editor of *Foreign Policy*) in paying close attention to Europe's problems, with Maynes considering U.S. policy options for containment of mounting ethnic warfare. Former Supreme Allied Commander for the North Atlantic, Admiral Paul David Miller (U.S. Navy) expands significantly on the role of American military power in providing secure environments in postauthoritarian, transitional systems.

Underlying such an organization and selection of contributors are two propositions. First, we maintain that the core of democracy's regeneration is an indigenous effort to expand the public political sphere, fostering a shift in political culture. Democracies cannot be made from above or generated from outside. The transformation of subjects into participants has no blueprint. Yet, democracies without an engaged citizenry are certain to be fleeting. Part I addresses these issues as they emerge in various societies.

Second, we consider that democracy may be security-dependent. Conditions in which personal or collective threats are absent, muted, or balanced by countervailing capacities enable democracy to be nurtured. The insecure do not become democrats, because pluralism, tolerance, and so on are

labeled as unaffordable luxuries when social, economic, or military catas-
trophe looms. Historically, democracies have developed and continued
almost without exception where some fortuitous security is provided by
geographic and resource abundance or a larger power's protection and
tutelage. The provision of security, via collective mechanisms, U.S. power
projection, or other means are options. In Part II, our contributors turn to
consider such matters.

Five years after the Berlin Wall fell, we see clear-cut signals that the
globalization of democracy is a distant goal, and that the "third wave" may
already be retreating from shore. No evidence thus far exists to reassure
anyone that remaining communist governments will soon *all* crumble, that
elections in West Africa will lead to popularly elected civilian governments
with a legitimate mandate, or that abusive dictatorial regimes in Myanmar
(Burma), Iraq, and elsewhere will be toppled. Instead, indications persist
that transnational threats emerging from decaying authoritarian regimes or
nascent postauthoritarian systems are afflicting and destabilizing entire
regions—with mass migrations, fear of covert arms transfers and proliferation, spreading ethnic strife, and other dangers.

The aftermath of authoritarianism, then, may be far less rewarding and
far more dangerous than we thought in 1989—it may be a precursor of a
new authoritarianism as the genesis of new threats undercuts the potential
for any sustained democratic transition.

Our effort to raise these issues for research and debate, and the subsequent publication of this volume, required enormous effort from the GPIS
Programs Coordinator, Ms. Elizabeth Thornton, and several staff members
who assisted with manuscript preparations. We are particularly grateful to
Ms. Ellen Libby and to a doctoral candidate, Ms. Juliet Thompson, for their
considerable assistance on this project. Mr. Thomas Lansford provided
additional help in manuscript preparation.

And, appreciation is also due to administrators and colleagues at Old
Dominion University who contributed resources and energies to this project, and to the first students and faculty of the Graduate Programs in
International Studies, without whose support this volume would have been
impossible.

NOTES

1. Amos Perlmutter, *Modern Authoritarianism* (New Haven, Conn.: Yale University Press, 1981), 24–28.

2. Larry Diamond, "The Globalization of Democracy: Trends, Types, Causes and Prospects," manuscript (1990).

3. This, of course, was Samuel Huntington's title, *The Third Wave: Democratization in the Late Twentieth Century* (Norman: University of Oklahoma Press, 1991).

4. Dankwart A. Rustow, "Transitions to Democracy: Toward a Dynamic Model," *Comparative Politics* (April 1970): 337.

Chapter 1

The Newer Democracies: From the Time of Triumph to the Time of Troubles

ROBERT A. DAHL

An astounding feature of our waning century has been the frequency of turnover in political regimes. Shifts between democratic governments and authoritarian rule, in both directions, have been numerous. Lately, as everyone knows, the democratic side has won a heartening string of victories: so many, indeed, that political leaders and pundits remind us tirelessly of "the victory of democracy"; we are instructed that we have now arrived at "the end of history"; and among scholars the subject of "transitions to democracy" has become a cottage industry, the focus of more scholarly conferences, articles, and monographs in this country and abroad than anyone can keep up with.

Yet among all these groups the celebratory mood is dampened by the growing realization that a transition to democracy may sometimes be followed by transition back to a nondemocratic system. Just as the preceding authoritarian regimes were beset with deep and persistent problems that undermined support for their rulers, so too many of the countries with new democratic governments face problems that weaken their support and strengthen their antidemocratic opponents. Consequently a goodly number have seen or are soon likely to see the beginning of a Time of Troubles. From this Time of Troubles some may not emerge with their democratic governments still in place.

We can gain some perspective on the speed and magnitude of the change if we contrast the situation today with that only four decades ago, the span of about two generations. In 1950 the full set of modern democratic political institutions mentioned earlier existed in about twenty-five countries, mainly the European or English-speaking countries that provide us with a reasonable minimal threshold. If we want to be strict about it and include universal suffrage as a democratic requirement, as we should, two otherwise fully democratic countries that I have counted among the twenty-five would have to be struck off, shocking though this might be to conventional usage and belief. Universal female suffrage in federal elections did not arrive in Switzerland until 1971; and painful as it is to recall, in parts of the United States, notably in the South, Blacks as we all know were not permitted to vote, in practice if not necessarily in law, until after the passage and enforcement of the civil rights legislation of the 1960s.

Moreover, among the twenty-five countries were several—Chile and Uruguay, for example—in which democracy would later break down and be replaced for some years by military dictatorship. We end up today, then, with a group of twenty-one countries (if we generously permit the United States and Switzerland to be counted among them) in which modern democratic political institutions have effectively and continuously existed since 1950 or earlier. Because these countries are very different in important ways from many that have acquired democratic governments since 1950, it is helpful to group them together as "older," more "stable," or "mature" democracies in order to distinguish them from the new democracies.

A count of the world's democracies today would show an extraordinary increase since 1950. Several years ago, after carefully examining the available evidence on 173 countries, two political scientists found that by the mid-1980s the number had almost doubled: by their measures there were twenty new full democracies in addition to the twenty-one surviving older ones.[1] Since their reckoning, four Latin American countries—Chile, Bolivia, Paraguay, and Nicaragua—have made the transition, bringing to at least twenty-five the number of countries in which democratic institutions, according to their criteria, have been newly introduced or reestablished. Using different criteria, a Finnish scholar recently put the total number of democracies at sixty-one in 1988.[2] Samuel Huntington, in his fine book *The Third Wave*, counted fifty-eight democratic countries in 1990, compared with twelve in 1942 and thirty in 1973.[3]

If we were to make a census today it would reveal still another increase, because all the estimates I have just given omit countries in Eastern Europe and the dismembered Soviet Union, where the inauguration of democratic political institutions has recently been completed or is in process. Nor do those numbers include a batch of countries whose governments cannot reasonably be called authoritarian and are ordinarily called democratic, like Israel and India, yet where one or more of the main democratic institutions is clearly below the threshold of the older democracies—where, for example, elections are sometimes badly tampered with or freedom of speech, press, or association is occasionally or even regularly impaired. Since no one seems to have come up with a noninvidious label for this group, perhaps for my purposes here they might be called near-democracies. Even by fairly strict political criteria, however, the new democracies are now more numerous than the old.

Many of the new democracies are, of course, extremely small countries—islands or, like Micronesia, collections of tiny islands and atolls. Among the countries that became democratic between 1950 and the mid-1980s, almost half had populations of a quarter million or less. Even if we omit countries with less than a million people, as Huntington does, the total number doubled from 1942 to 1990. (One of the countries thus omitted, by the way, is Iceland, where democracy is probably as deeply rooted in history and culture as anywhere in the world.)

Given the unprecedented number of democratic countries in the world today, it may come as a surprise that the *proportion* of democratic and nondemocratic countries has not shown a corresponding increase: the proportion with fully democratic governments is surprisingly close to what it was in 1950.[4] The explanation for this seeming paradox is simply that the number of nominally independent countries in the world has also greatly increased: from around 75 countries in 1950 to around 170 in the mid-1980s. Since the 1980s the breakup of the Soviet Union into 15 republics together with the merging of East Germany into the Federal Republic has produced a net increase of 13 countries, for a total that is edging toward the 200 mark. Thus while the number of democracies has greatly increased, so has the number of countries, leaving the proportion roughly the same.

Even so, employing a global perspective we are surely entitled to celebrate this Time of Triumph for democracy. But triumphs, alas, are sometimes followed by defeats. It is sobering to recall that while "transitions to democracy" is now a hot topic among historians and political scientists, only a few years ago scholars were devoting about as much attention to the task of understanding why democracies fail. To the older and much-studied (though not all that well understood) cases of Italy, Germany, Austria, and Spain, later decades added the breakdowns in Latin America of Argentina, Brazil, Colombia, Peru, Venezuela, Chile, and Uruguay (among others) and elsewhere in the world Turkey, Lebanon, Greece, the Philippines, Pakistan, and others, including a slew of African countries, some having high promise like Nigeria. A British political scientist has counted fifty-two cases in which nondemocratic regimes replaced democratic governments between 1900 and 1985 (excluding the destruction of democratic governments because of foreign invasion and occupation).[5] In the book I have already referred to, Samuel Huntington points out that each of the two preceding waves of democratization was followed by a reverse wave. A long wave of democratization running from 1828 to 1926 was followed by a reverse wave from 1922 to 1942; a second short wave from 1943 to 1962 had already begun to collapse by 1958; the third wave began only in 1974.[6] Is the third wave, like its predecessors, about to recede? From its Time of Triumph is democracy now heading into its Time of Troubles?

DISTINCTIVE FEATURES OF DEMOCRATIC GOVERNMENT

Before responding to that question, I want to engage in a brief digression. Since any statement employing the words *democratic* and *nondemocratic* immediately invites challenge, let me pause to make clear what I mean by a democratic government.

What distinguishes modern democratic systems both from nondemocratic regimes and also from premodern democracies and republics is a distinctive constellation of political institutions that effectively (and not just nominally) exist within a country. These include the selection of top officials in free and fair elections, extensive freedom of expression, wide access to alternative and independent sources of information, rights to form relatively independent associations and organizations, including political parties entitled to compete in elections, and an inclusive electorate. Note that it is the simultaneous presence of all these institutions that makes modern democratic governments so distinctive. This historically unique combination of political institutions has become so familiar to us that we easily forget a simple historical fact: while some aspects of these institutions were present in the few democracies and republics that existed before the nineteenth century, in its entirety this particular set of political practices and arrangements was foreign to the theory and practice of democratic and republican government, and virtually unimaginable for two thousand years.

Indeed, while most of these political institutions began to make their appearance in a comparatively small number of countries during the nineteenth century, one of them, universal adult suffrage, did not even then become a part of the standard theory and practice of democracy. With the single exception of New Zealand the national franchise was nowhere guaranteed to women until this century. In most of the otherwise democratic countries, in fact, women did not gain the suffrage until after World War I: in Belgium and France not until after World War II—and, as I have mentioned, in Switzerland not until 1971! Thus modern democracy, at least if it is defined by the full set of political institutions I just described, is distinctly a creation of the twentieth century, a fact that suggests the following arresting thought: even in the oldest existing democracies (New Zealand perhaps excepted) democracy in the full-fledged modern sense is younger than its oldest living citizens.

In speaking of the recent triumphs of democracy, then, I am referring to the dramatic increase in the number of countries in which the full constel- lation of political institutions mentioned above exists at or above the threshold levels established in this century in Western Europe and the main English-speaking countries (with the exception of South Africa).

It may be hard to grasp just how different the recent string of democratic victories has made the time in which we now live. Yet a fundamental fact of the 1990s is that the strength of democratic ideas and practices in the world today means that the period in which we are now living is, quite literally, historically unique. Never before in human history have demo- cratic political institutions so widely prevailed. Considered in the long perspective of world history, the significance of this change can hardly be exaggerated. The recent rapid march of modern democratic institutions across the globe may cause us to forget that until this century belief in the democratic idea and widespread support for political practices intended to embody it in actual governments could be found only in a few places and among a small minority of the world's population. Today around one-fifth of the people in the world live in countries with fully democratic govern- ments. Perhaps nearly as many live in countries with nearly democratic governments. To this total, the people of what used to be called Eastern Europe and the Soviet Union could add nearly an additional 10 percent.

Except for the oil sheikdoms, the richest countries in the world all have democratic governments. Democratic countries account for a preponderant proportion of the world's trade, manufacturing, and output of goods and services. They have no significant competitors in military strength, strategic position, and influence over the thinking and behavior of the people of the world.

What is even more striking is the near collapse of antidemocratic ideolo- gies. This, too, is historically unique and yet all too easily forgotten. Democracy's older rivals, which prevailed in most of the world throughout most of recorded history, such as monarchy, hereditary aristocracy, narrow oligarchy, even a representative government with a highly restricted, property-based suffrage, had already lost their punch by the end of World War I. Today the newer rivals, more populist in content, are also out of the game. The appeal of Nazi and fascist ideologies precipitously collapsed in the ruins of their regimes. As a believable ideology, authoritarian Marxism, whether Leninist, Maoist, or Castroite, is so close to death that I cannot imagine how it will ever be resuscitated. Argentina's peculiar populist-authoritarian ideology, Peronism, has been domesticated; whatever may occur in that troubled country, a massive return to true-believer Peronism seems unlikely.

In Latin America, the political, military, economic, or moral failures of military dictatorships—in some cases all of these together—have brought the idea of military rule into disrepute. While military takeovers may well occur, indeed probably will occur, military rule as such has little ideological appeal. In any case, Latin American military regimes failed to create a genuine ideological alternative that would persist after their downfall. In fact, military dictatorships in Latin America have rarely if ever explicitly rejected the ideal of democratic or republican government as such; instead they typically represented themselves as regimes of limited term, necessary for public order, suppressing terror, and the destruction of communism or other enemies, until such time as democratic government could be safely restored.

On a global scale, perhaps the only major ideological alternatives at present are nationalism and Islamic fundamentalism. In the past, democracy and a strong sense of nationhood have more often been allies than enemies. On the other hand, reactionary nationalists are usually prepared, even eager, to sacrifice democratic institutions to their goal of excluding, expelling, or extirpating those who live within the country and yet are defined by them as outside the "real" nation. Because of its theocratic elements Islamic fundamentalism may also prove to be incompatible with democracy in both theory and practice. Important as it now is, however, the future of Islamic fundamentalism will be confined to predominantly Islamic countries, and not all of those.

DEMOCRACY'S TIME OF TROUBLES?

So has the world at last been made safe for democracy? Surely much safer than it has ever been in recorded human history. But in many countries where it has recently been inaugurated democracy is still a very risky business.

I have already suggested that on a global scale, democracy may now be passing from its Time of Triumph to its Time of Troubles. The metaphor may also help us as we think about recent transitions from authoritarianism to democracy in particular countries. A country moving to democracy wins its first victory when the long dark night of authoritarian rule is brought to an end and democratic forces gain control over the state. This is a Time of Hope. In a second victory, democratic political institutions and a democratic constitution are established, or in some countries reestablished. This second victory often inaugurates a triumphal period, an exhilarating moment when the old chronic fears abate, people exuberantly exercise their new freedoms, and the corrupt, oppressive, mean, and dangerous politics of authoritarianism is briefly replaced by a politics of solidarity, decency, dedication, and public spiritedness. New leaders who appear to embody the hopeful spirit and the nobility of the new politics—Alfonsín, Aquino, Havel—seem to speak directly to the hearts of their people; and many citizens in the older democracies express regret because these new and purer voices contrast so sharply with the stale rhetoric and narrow interest-group demands of their own politicians. Though in the exhilaration of victory this Time of Triumph gives promise of enduring indefinitely, it often turns out instead to be a comparatively short and easy period.

All too soon the time will inevitably arrive when stubborn, even intractable problems—political, economic, social, international—have to be confronted. For any regime this is a dangerous time. It is certain to be so for a new democracy as it moves from the Time of Triumph to the Time of Troubles.

Just how dangerous a time is suggested by the frequency of democratic breakdowns, which I mentioned earlier. What is striking, however, is how extraordinarily rare it has been for democracy to give way to an authoritarian regime in countries where the main institutions have been in place for some time. Of the fifty-two cases of breakdown that I cited a moment ago, all but two (Uruguay and Chile) occurred in countries where fully democratic institutions had not existed for more than twenty years (and because of the very late arrival of an extended suffrage, even Chile is a less clear-cut case than its democratic experience would otherwise suggest). It is not in the "older" or "mature" democracies that democratic breakdowns have occurred. The problem is primarily one for new democracies.

We should not be altogether surprised, then, if the future repeats the past and democracy gives way to nondemocratic governments in several of the new democracies or if some of the near-democracies, like India, retrogress to less democratic forms of rule.

BREAKDOWN OF DEMOCRACY

Why is democracy likely to break down in some countries? The reasons are, I fear, all too obvious. To begin with, a fair number of the newly created democratic and protodemocratic governments exist in countries that are themselves newly created. As a consequence, they often confront the usual obstacles of new countries in achieving national integration in the face of existing and often ancient linguistic, ethnic, religious, or regional conflicts, which are sometimes compounded by ideological differences. Moreover, many newly democratic countries are also sorely beset with acute economic problems. In most, average incomes are low—much lower, certainly, than in the opulent older democratic countries: in the mid-1980s GNP per capita among the new democracies was on average about one-fifth that of the older democracies. In many countries, poverty is widespread, along with the social and physical problems associated with poverty. Even where people enjoy higher standards of living, as in Argentina, their demands and expectations are also higher; and governments may fail to fulfill their own promises of economic growth and prosperity. In many countries, of course, the economy is weighed down even further by the staggering weight of foreign debt. And a fair number of the brand-new microstates, the islands in the Caribbean and the Pacific, are almost totally dependent on outsiders for their security and economic survival.

Several large countries, like Peru and Colombia, are torn by massive terrorism and violence. Indeed, with its terrorism, acute economic difficulties, and urban crime, Peru, once a county of enormous vitality and promise, has become the most intractable case in the Western Hemisphere. In some less stricken countries, like Honduras and Guatemala, the military in effect exercises an implicit veto over the conduct of the government. Elections may be fair enough, but elected leaders well know that they dare not overstep boundaries set by the military. In other countries—Argentina, Brazil, Chile, and Uruguay come to mind—civilian governments have had to search for an accommodation with the past that will neither provoke the military nor perpetuate the memory of its injustices. That is no easy task.

In countries with deeply rooted democratic cultures, some of these difficulties might be less threatening to democratic stability. In the older democracies, democratic values, beliefs, practices, and habits are typically products of a lengthy historical growth long antecedent to the actual arrival of the full array of political institutions mentioned earlier. To be sure, even in these older democracies democratic beliefs often seem superficial or fragile, and the discrepancy between publicly avowed beliefs and actual practices can be appalling. Nonetheless, the democratic cultures of these countries have proven strong enough to see them through severe crises that would have brought down less deeply rooted democratic systems. In most of the newer democracies, however, democratic beliefs and practices have not yet had the time to deepen their roots. Prolonged crisis is the last thing they need.

Four of the countries of Central America provide an extreme example. Of the forty-seven governments that came to power in Guatemala, El Salvador, Honduras, and Nicaragua between 1948 and 1982, over two-thirds gained power by means other than free and fair elections: most frequently by a military coup, and in several instances through fraudulent elections. Three-fourths of these governments were headed by military leaders or a junta of military leaders and civilians.[7] This appalling historical record—which after all is only the tail end of a much longer record—is hardly an experience conducive to the development of a widespread democratic culture.

To Tocqueville a century and a half ago, time was definitely on the side of equality and democracy. He has proven to be essentially correct. But given the acute problems many of the new democracies and protodemocracies face, in the intermediate term—a generation or so—time may not be on the side of democracy. In an adverse climate, the green and shallow roots of the democratic culture needed to sustain democratic political institutions may shrivel and die. New antidemocratic ideologies, probably with a strongly populist and pseudodemocratic rhetoric, will surely arise. Persistent economic hardship accompanied by corruption and public disorder may even make the discredited alternative of military rule seem more appealing.

FIVE CONDITIONS FOR STABLE DEMOCRACY

The prospects for achieving greater democratization and ultimately a stable democratic system depend, of course, on the particular conditions of a country. Because these vary over a tremendous range, countries vary enormously in their prospects. They vary not only in the degree to which elements of the democratic political institutions are already present, but also in the background conditions that favor or damage the prospects for democratization.

Five background conditions are particularly weighty. I have already stressed the crucial place of democratic beliefs and democratic culture. Beliefs and cultures do not grow up overnight or exist as disembodied entities independent of a country's past and present. Obviously, however, they bear heavily on democratic prospects. Given the prior experience of democracy in Chile and Uruguay before their military takeovers and the strength of their democratic cultures, even in the darkest days of military rule it was a reasonable guess that full democracy would be restored in these countries before it would arrive in, say, Taiwan or South Korea.

As these examples suggest, a country's past and present include a second factor, the importance of which is testified to by the frequency of military coups and military dictatorships: the main instruments of violent coercion, the military and police, must be so firmly under the control of elected civilian leaders that they cannot be employed to gain or maintain domination over the state. Even so, as Chile and Uruguay illustrate again, extreme polarization can pave the way for the military to take over as the ostensible guarantors of public order.

Therefore the likelihood of democratic stability is higher if there is moderate homogeneity, that is, a lack of sharply differentiated, ingrown subcultures focused on religion, ethnic groupings, race, language, or ideology. Where cleavages like these are present, as they have been in a few of the older democracies, democratic stability may be achieved by special arrangements for conciliation, accommodation, and consensus (which some political scientists call "consociational democracy")—as in Switzerland and Belgium, for example.

The prospects for democracy in the present-day world are also enormously greater in countries marked by certain characteristics that we have come to associate with modernity: societies and economies that encourage social and organizational pluralism; market economies; historically high levels of wealth and income, consumption, literacy, and education; increasing rather than static or declining standards of living, and so on.

Even in a country where all the favorable conditions I have mentioned so far are present, democratic institutions could still be impaired or destroyed, of course, by the harsh intervention of a foreign power hostile to democratization. Czechoslovakia furnishes a poignant example: had that country been free of Soviet domination, surely it would be numbered today among the older democracies, instead of emerging only recently with the heavy burdens of a new democracy weighed down even further by the need to transform its obsolete centralized socialist economy into a decentralized market economy.

Though no one of these conditions is sufficient by itself to ensure that a country will possess democratic political institutions, the odds are extremely high that a country will be democratic if all are present, and negligible if all are lacking. Where some are present and other weak or missing, the outcome is chancy. It is particularly in such countries that outside help and encouragement can sometimes make a difference.

POLICY IMPLICATIONS

How and how much we in the older democracies, especially the United States, can and should do to assist the development and stability of democracy elsewhere is a question so perplexing as to make one skeptical of simple answers. Rather than attempting an answer here I want to offer some guidelines for thinking one's way toward sensible answers.

- Democratization depends far less on what outsiders can do than on what the leaders and people within the country can and will do.

- What they are capable of doing, and likely to do, in turn depends greatly on the background conditions I described a moment ago. These are resistant to quick and peaceful change.

- Because these background conditions vary enormously from one country to another, no general strategy of democratization is feasible. More specifically, the prospects for any given country should be appraised with the particular features of that country clearly in mind: its history, the specific nature of the background conditions, the concrete character of its existing political institutions, and so on.

- If a primary aim of American policy is democratization, if structural changes are necessary for democratic political institutions to function effectively, and if the people in a country cannot or will not bring about these necessary changes, even with outside assistance, then the United States cannot accomplish its aim and should either withdraw its assistance or change its goal.

- A patient, steady, persistent, long-run American policy of providing appropriate support for democratization when the opportunities arise—however marginal these opportunities may be at the time—could make a difference. We have never steadily adhered to such a policy in the past. Even if we were to pursue such a policy in the future, some of the new democracies might still undergo authoritarian takeovers. But our actions could increase the chances that they will ride out their Times of Troubles and in due course become stable democratic countries.

- Finally, wherever feasible the United States should act in concert with other democratic countries, preferably through multilateral organizations. After World

War II many Americans came to see their country as exceptional in the strength not only of its commitment to democracy but also of its economic, military, and diplomatic resources, and consequently in its capacity for fostering democratic development, elsewhere. That flattering self-image was at best always a serious distortion of reality. Attempts by the United States to influence the internal affairs of other countries have sometimes impeded rather than fostered democratic development. Indeed, in Latin America our long-term record is, despite a few exceptions, abysmal. By acting in concert with other democratic countries, the United States is more likely to support rather than weaken democratic prospects, and also to participate in a more effective effort.

Earlier I mentioned the extraordinary preponderance in wealth and power of democratic countries today, together with the drastic decline in much of the world, for the time being at least, in the legitimacy of ideological or constitutional alternatives to democratic governments. This historically unique situation fundamentally alters one of the major background conditions for democracy: the influence of foreign powers. Today for the first time in world history the preponderant international influence throughout most of the globe is on the side of democratic ideas and institutions. Multilateral actions to foster fledgling democratic institutions, such as protecting fundamental human rights or free and fair elections, are becoming commonplace on the international scene. Although this change does not and cannot ensure that democracy will evolve or survive in a country where the background conditions are highly adverse, in a country where the conditions are more favorable joint action by democratic countries could sometimes significantly increase the likelihood of democratic development.

CONCLUSION

It is beyond the power and resources of the United States and other democratic countries to ensure that new democracies will everywhere survive. In some countries the survival of democracy is likely to be, at best, a rather risky matter. But we can sometimes act to better the odds. In a world of high uncertainty, I am fairly confident at least of this: if new democracies collapse in part because we in the older democracies fail to provide the crucial support they need during their Times of Troubles, later generations will surely condemn us, and rightly so, for our own deficiencies in political judgment and moral strength.

NOTES

1. Michael Coppage and Wolfgang Reinicke, "A Scale of Polyarchy," in Raymond D. Gastil, *Freedom in the World: Political Rights and Civil Liberties, 1987–1988* (Lanham, Md.: University Press of America, 1988), 101–125.

2. Tatu Vanhanen, *The Process of Democratization: A Comparative Study of 147 States, 1980–88* (New York: Crane Russak, 1990).

3. Samuel Huntington, *The Third Wave: Democratization in the Late Twentieth Century* (Norman: University of Oklahoma Press, 1991), Table 1.1, 26. He omits countries with a population of less than one million.

4. By my count, around one-third, give or take a few percentage points. Omitting the smaller countries, Huntington found that the percentage of democracies in 1990 was virtually identical with what it was in 1922—45 percent. Huntington, *The Third Wave*, Table 1.1, 26.

5. Frank Bealey, "Stability and Crisis: Fears about Threats to Democracy," *European Journal of Political Research* 15 (1987): 687–715.

6. Huntington, *The Third Wave*, 16.

7. Mark Rosenberg, "Political Obstacles to Democracy in Central America," in James M. Malloy and Mitchell Seligson, eds., *Authoritarian and Democratic Transitions in Latin America* (Pittsburgh: University of Pittsburgh, 1987), 193–250.

Part I

Opposing Authoritarianism, Building Democracy: Case Studies

In past epochs, the genesis of democracy lay in anticolonial struggles or social revolutions. Today, efforts to broaden the public political sphere and to increase social tolerance and other tenets ascribed to democracy require, first, overcoming institutionalized authoritarianism.

Much more than throwing off the shackles of foreign oppressors or of an aristocratic class, building democracy at the end of the twentieth century necessitates a strategy to undermine and weaken a well-entrenched authoritarian bureaucracy. Whether led by an ideological party of the left, an army-business junta of the right, or other variants, control embedded in the bureaucracy has reinforced and sometimes supplanted ecclesiastical endorsement, or sheer terror. Manipulation of information, regulation of rewards and punishments, and denial of associational freedom are the daily "stuff" of modern authoritarian systems.

But overcoming these behavioral constraints is only the first step. Then, notwithstanding the exhaustion created by authoritarian rigidity, today's democratizers must dismantle the institutions of control, and build new, responsive structures that operate within the rule of law.

These lengthy processes offer no guarantee of success. Yet, the large-scale, violent events that were political supernovas of the past were also no insurance of positive outcomes. Among the greatest anticolonial struggles and the largest social revolutions, one finds a dubious record without much long-term commitment to revolutionary values or movement toward democracy.

Popular effort and sacrifice are at the core of late-twentieth-century challenges to the rule of one party, one class, or one belief. Democracy, if it means anything, connotes a popularly legitimized government. Rather than specific institutional or procedural requisites, attributes of a democracy are subjective. Popular will is essential for an open, tolerant, and competitive system, regardless of whether it is generated by charismatic leadership, by abject suffering, or by a sense of national indignity. International pressure cannot democratize.

In Part I, four case studies exemplify the most critical component of late-twentieth-century challenges to authoritarianism and the reconstitution of democracy—the human component. Citizenship is the key to a system's democratic capacity; without an expansion of the public political sphere, authoritarian systems cannot be challenged. And, unless popular participation is maintained, freedoms, tolerance, and competition can be pushed aside with ease.

In four quite different environments, the dynamics of democratization are discussed, and prognoses assessed. In three cases, notable participants in the struggle to renew democracy in their countries present analyses of their own success or failure. Former Argentine president Raúl Alfonsín valiantly sought to restore his country's democracy in the aftermath of a vicious period of military rule. Alfonsín's efforts paid off, even if not to his own political fortunes. As with Alfonsín, Liu Binyan's name is almost instantly recognizable; among Chinese who were politically aware in the 1960s and 1970s, Liu became a strong advocate of democratic reform even while still in China and suffering because of his views. Floribert Chebeya fights on against Zaïre's dictator, Mobutu, and conducts a gallant day-to-day effort to keep the world aware of that struggle. Concerning postcommunist Europe, the Nelson chapter develops a theoretical perspective on *how* the public political sphere widens and why that process is vital for breaking away from authoritarianism.

In these different settings, then, the complexities of late-twentieth-century democratization are explored. And, despite many regional and country-specific differences, the forces available to authoritarians today cannot be attacked with a simplistic antiforeign or anticlass strategy. Instead, the notion of "people power"—of national empowerment—is key. Authoritarianism fails and can be swept away only when the popular demand for change overwhelms those in power. Sadly, we have seen only a faint glimmer of that struggle in most of the world.

Chapter 2

The Transition toward Democracy in a Developing Country: The Case of Argentina

RAÚL ALFONSÍN

A FOUNDATION FOR DEMOCRACY

People who live under dictatorships often experience order as an imposition and dissent as an unnatural perturbance; as a result they can lose their aptitude for dialogue, negotiation, and compromise.[1] When we took office in 1983,[2] we knew that to build democracy we had to overcome these authoritarian tendencies that were shared to different degrees by all of us, even by those who were deeply committed to democracy; for the dangers to the democratic way of life are not posed exclusively by the strength and force of its acknowledged enemies—they can also be found within ourselves. We had all experienced the threat of violence, distrust and indifference; our traditions of solidarity weakened as we took refuge in our personal lives, and that isolation added to the political vacuum in which we lived.

On taking office one of our principal goals was to regain trust in one another and in our institutions by rebuilding our sense of community. Given the deep wounds and fears left on the body politic by the violence of the recent past,[3] it was not a simple project and the attempt to carry it out took its toll on our government.

We did have one advantage: fanatical convictions had lost favor. This meant that few believed in messianic movements or entertained the hope that happiness could be assured through one violent episode that would magically bring about change and give birth to a new form of life, whether by terrorism or war. Most of us knew that building democracy was a difficult enterprise and that it would take a long time to complete.

We were concerned about how modernization fits in a democracy because we did not believe that democracy can take hold just by engineering changes in the economy. True, democracy requires modernization: a profound progressive change in the social order, but a change that must temper technological advance with humane social values and respect for the community. Modernization, understood exclusively as social-economic change made exclusively to reduce costs, encourage competition, and increase profits—or bring about socialism—is narrow-minded and at odds with the respect for human beings which is at the foundation of a democratic society. We did not want to discard criteria of efficiency—that would have been suicide. We wanted to guide their use with humane values so they might harmonize with the social and economic security required by consumers and workers, understanding that this harmony enhances opportunity rather than holds it back in a modern society. We were wary of the authoritarian processes of modernization, and we did not want these processes to undermine our democracy.[4]

We were also aware that the crises of the first few cycles of modernization in this century had revealed the political weakness of that process. Modernization and industrialization stitch together processes of incomplete social and economic change in which each transformation is encrusted on top of that which came before it. Society develops as a sum of social aggregates which make demands on the state. In this way society becomes increasingly fragmented and blocked into self-serving corporations, and the state, overburdened by the competing sectoral claims, is paralyzed by the rules and regulations it sanctions to provide successive privileged regimes for these groups. Fascism was an extreme authoritarian response to the social, political, and economic consequences of a process of modernization unrestrained by respect for, and solidarity with, the individual human being.[5]

We wanted a flexible society rather than a blocked one. Obviously we did not expect to dissolve all elements of order and social discipline that are accepted by consensus and that constitute the structure of civilized life. Flexibility does not mean anomie. We wanted to acknowledge and promote a public dimension as one of the key components of democracy,[6] distinct and different from both the sphere of private interests and the dominion of the state.

For all these reasons we tried to base our democracy on an ethic of solidarity defining a set of social and political rights for which all citizens would feel obliged to struggle regardless of the group or social sector to which they belonged. The right to freely express one's ideas, for example, is only an abstraction unless it is guaranteed by the right to have an education which develops the capacity to entertain, develop, and compare ideas; the right to free association is vacuous, if ten, twelve, or fourteen hours of work are required for an individual to assure his or her subsistence, leaving no time or energy to meet others to discuss public affairs; and the right to one's life and liberty is meaningless if a judicial system does not credibly protect those rights against the state or terrorists.

In the past many attempts to establish democracy failed, either because people did not believe that democracy could improve their condition or because they were not allowed to participate in the processes of creating a democratic society.[7] Our goal in Argentina in 1983 was to avoid these failures. We did not simply want to govern, we wanted to help build, protect, and consolidate the democratic spirit of our people. We set out to accomplish this task in very difficult times and trying circumstances. What follows is a summary of the main obstacles we faced and an account of some of our accomplishments and failures.

OBSTACLES

After a period of brilliant development that began in the last part of the nineteenth century and lasted until 1930,[8] Argentina fell into a state of economic stagnation and political authoritarianism. During the fifty-three years from 1930 to 1983 politics in Argentina developed in a climate that encouraged and rewarded direct action, the illegal shortcut, and explicit or implicit violence. The many *coups d'état* in this period had an important role in promoting this climate. I should point out that it is a simplification to define these coups as military coups when in reality they have always relied on civilians. The military responsibility for the operational aspects of a coup should not blind us to the heavy responsibility borne by those civilians who programmed the coups, provided their ideology, and in many cases inspired them.[9] Military rule has not been the only cause of our problems, but it certainly is one of their most obvious symptoms.

Violence and direct action were encouraged by fraudulent practices; the abuse of power even promoted the idea that the majority could override the rights of the minority, and these practices extended into the economic system at a crucial stage of its development. This climate of lawlessness explains how terrorism arose in the 1970s as one of the most cruel and bloody forms of direct action, and it explains the military government's illegal response to terrorism. The rule of law was not credible and therefore if a person had the power, anything was possible.

This climate of lawlessness, which had encouraged both terrorism and government counterterrorism in Argentina, was one of the main obstacles we had to overcome. We attempted to change this climate by bringing to justice the people most responsible for subversive terrorism and state terrorism. It was an unprecedented policy which was very difficult to implement because it did not satisfy special interest groups on the left, who thought it weak and unfair, and it stirred unrest in parts of the military that felt threatened by it. I believe the policy worked and helped transform our political culture by raising respect for the rule of law. Its success is one of the reasons Argentina has now been a democracy for eleven years, for the first time since 1930.

The other great obstacle we faced was the economy. When I was inaugurated, inflation had reached a yearly rate of 400 percent; the fiscal deficit was 15 percent of the gross national product (GNP); the external debt, calculated at $46 billion, required 63 percent of the country's internal savings for servicing, which totaled 69 percent of our exports; the social security system was fiscally bankrupt; public investment commitments were underfinanced; public sector productivity was low and falling; the central government's financial relations with the provinces were in disarray; and the nation's reserves were only at $102 million.

The economic situation was worsened by the international foreign debt crisis, which did not seem to have a solution. In the case of Argentina international credit had not been contracted to acquire capital goods and technology, nor to improve the productive sector of the economy. The money had left the country through capital flight, through spending by Argentine tourists abroad, and by the acquisition of unnecessary luxury imports. The international nature of the debt crisis, which seemed to imperil the stability of the financial system of the Western powers, limited our chances of obtaining foreign investments needed for growth and employment. The economy stagnated and social tensions worsened.

For domestic policy reasons interest rates in the developed countries, especially the United States, were high and continued to be high during the 1980s in an effort to control inflation in the industrialized world. That restrictive monetary policy had a devastating effect on debt service since we paid interest on the debt at market rates charged in the United States and Europe.

It will always remain a bitter paradox for us that the advanced industrial democracies which encouraged us to consolidate our democratic institutions at the same time discriminated against us in trade, subsidizing their agricultural exports (which were our main source of hard currency for repaying the debt) so that they would be unfairly competitive against ours, and demanding debt repayment at the very high interest rates required by their exclusively domestically oriented monetary policies. Another disappointment was the conditionality multilateral international lending institutions placed on their loans. On many occasions these institutions held back credit, or disbursements, until we met conditions of dubious practicality or benefit.[10]

We also were hurt by the logic of the Cold War, which divided the world between the good and the bad and the submitted and the rebellious. To achieve our objectives we needed peace and a world order in which the struggle between the powerful would be replaced by cooperation, and in which the priorities of freedom, justice, and development would displace the arms race. Today these goals inspire the main protagonists of the international order; in 1983 they were not even present in their dreams.

THE RESULTS

With respect to the economy we carried out a reasonably balanced economic plan for the short and middle term that included an innovative formula to stop inflation without sacrificing the principle of equality. We hoped to finance government operations without printing money and to obtain a surplus to help finance interest payments on the foreign debt. This plan was conceived as the first of a series of reforms aimed at integrating Argentina within the world economy. We discarded the nominal fixed exchange rate, used active rules of intervention in the economy, including the control of prices and salaries, and managed differential exchange rates. We promoted private investment in risky ventures in traditionally public areas of the economy as a move toward privatization, and to finance new investments we created a system for accepting bids for anticipated cancellation of the foreign debt. We established a stable financial relation between the nation and the provinces, attacked the financial crisis of the pension system by creating new taxes that provided 40 percent of its income, and exposed the hidden nature of some state subsidies by including them in the budget.

But when all was said and done the facts proved that we did not do enough. Acting independently of the different sectors of the economy, the government was not able to overcome its isolation and failed to discipline the corporations. The private sector refused to increase production without increasing prices; in many cases it did not pay taxes and chose to import rather than export. Finally, in the last six months of our government our economic policy broke down under the pressure of political events. When the polls started to show that the opposition candidate, who had promised to simultaneously increase salaries, diminish taxes, and freeze the cost of basic services was going to win, the bottom fell out of the economy. The exchange rate went through the roof, inflation returned with greater virulence, no one invested, and hardly anyone paid taxes.

In foreign affairs we worked for peace and justice and recovered the international prestige of the republic, advanced in processes of regional integration, and defended in every forum the principles of international law. During my administration we settled the dispute with Chile over islands in the Beagle Channel which had almost led to war in 1978. The nuclear rivalry with Brazil was carefully transformed into a relationship of cooperation in research. We began Mercosur—a working project of a free trade zone in the southern cone. We were able to demonstrate that dialogue, negotiations and compromise with our neighbors, offered more benefits than rivalry and war.

Great strides were made in the modernization of society in terms of extending and deepening the rule of law: the rights of women were affirmed and values which allowed for tolerance and compromise were consolidated. During my government divorce and remarriage were legalized, and women were given the same rights and responsibilities with respect to their offspring as men. We also advanced in other areas such as education, but this is not the place for a listing of these accomplishments.

A SPECIAL CASE: HUMAN RIGHTS

During the dictatorship (1976–1983) thousands of citizens were arrested without legal warrant, and as part of the military government's response to a terrorist campaign that killed more than one thousand persons in the 1970s, thousands of those taken in this manner were secretly and systematically tortured and assassinated in numerous detention centers;[11] they were known as the "disappeared."

In Argentina the crimes of *de facto* governments were never punished, and in the last democratic interlude (1973–1976), terrorists had been forgiven and let out of jail. In 1983 our government broke these precedents, prosecuting those most responsible for state terrorism and subversive terrorism[12] and creating a national commission formed by distinguished persons from all walks of life to investigate the disappearances and provide an account of the tragedy to the community.[13]

Our aim was more to prevent and educate than to punish, while expunging the notion deeply ingrained in the body politic that people of high rank enjoyed legal impunity. We wanted to internalize in the collective conscience of the nation the idea that no group, however powerful, could consider itself above the law and sacrifice human lives to achieve its aims, however valuable they might seem. We wanted to uphold and dignify the rule of law.

Our policy objectives were shared by the majority of the people, who were awakening from their night of terror, but they were opposed by those who still believed that crimes were only committed on one side and that on "their side" there were only idealists who were guilty only of excusable "excesses" committed for a good cause, even when these "excesses" included the systematic torture and assassination of suspects or blowing up a mess hall of military officers and civilians.

To implement our policy we had to keep the armed forces loyal to democracy by demonstrating to them we were not questioning their legitimate role in our nation. To that end we distinguished clearly and forcefully between the legality of a frontal and open fight against subversion, and the clandestine and systematic torture and assassination of unarmed prisoners. We tried to restrain the public commotion (*estrepito fori*) caused by the trial of high-ranking military officers and to limit the length of the procedures and the categories of persons that would be held responsible. This is one reason why, during my campaign for president, we insisted on the distinction between those who conceived and gave the orders in the state's repressive apparatus, or exceeded their mandate in following orders, and those officers, servicemen, and policemen who, operating in a climate of terror and compulsion and lacking the capacity to make decisions, simply carried them out.

The military dictatorship had passed the so-called law of "self-amnesty" toward the end of its rule to cover up its own abuses and those of left-wing terrorism,[14] hoping that our democratic government would accept their trade-off with the leaders of the terrorists, an acceptance that would have started us on the wrong foot in establishing the rule of law in Argentina. So we passed through Congress a law that declared the self-amnesty law null *ab initio*,[15] on the grounds that the validity of the statutes enacted by a *de facto* government is precarious because these statutes violate Article 29 of the Constitution, which prohibits the concentration of power in one branch of government, and Article 16 of the Constitution, which guarantees equal protection of the law. Had we not annulled that law of the Junta, the trials of military officers suspected of violating human rights and of suspected terrorists would have been impossible because Argentine jurisprudence states that when a law changes after a criminal act, the accused must be judged according to the law most beneficial to the defendant.

It should be noted that it was essential to our purpose to proceed, and be perceived as proceeding, according to legal procedure step-by-step and respecting Constitutional practice; the heart of our purpose was to demonstrate to the people of Argentina that only respect for the rule of law could ensure that the evils of the past would be condemned and that they would be protected from such crimes in the future. In Argentina, the military justice system had jurisdiction over crimes committed by the military, and we could not simply bypass that system by handing the cases over to the civilian courts. Doing so would have run the risk of violating the Constitutional guarantee that an accused cannot be taken from the jurisdiction of the judges assigned to him by law, though many people suggested that course of action. We accepted an intermediate solution: the accused would be tried by military courts subject to civilian court review. We also had to decide legally whether junior officers and servicemen were responsible for crimes committed by following orders issued by their commanders. The executive proposed an interpretation of "due obedience" according to which, given the special circumstances of pressure, propaganda, and terror under which the crimes were committed, military personnel who followed orders, and did not have the capacity to make decisions, acted under the presumption of making an unavoidable mistake.

Within this legal framework we brought to trial all the superior officers who formed the three military juntas that governed Argentina between 1976 and 1982.[16] But as we were doing this we were fully aware of the need to limit the trials in duration and as to the number of the accused. We wanted to finish as quickly as possible with this matter and put it behind us, but without sacrificing our stated purposes: to morally and legally condemn the crimes, punish those most responsible for having them committed, and strengthen the rule of law in the country.

The trials lasted a long time, too long, for two reasons. First, the Supreme Council of the Armed Forces, under whose jurisdiction the trial began, after stalling proceedings for many months, resigned *en masse*, forcing the civilian courts to try the cases according the Code of Military Justice. Second, the Senate modified the concept of "due obedience" in our original legislative proposal so that it could not excuse atrocious and aberrant acts,[17] a modification that opened the door to unlimited prosecutions.

This turn of events added fuel to a never-ending psychological campaign that led to a grave state of unrest in the armed forces. Many officers felt threatened by the trials. This motivated the government to introduce a legislative proposal in 1986 to limit the time available to prosecute military and law enforcement officers on human rights violations committed during the dictatorship.[18] This law was passed by Congress, but it had a counter-productive effect by establishing a time limit which accelerated the development of new cases and encouraged the activation of cases that were languishing in the courts in order to beat the deadline. The number of court subpoenas and procedures to which the military was submitted increased dramatically the scope of the proceedings and the unrest in the armed forces.

On Easter weekend in 1987,[19] core sectors of the armed forces mutinied. The mutiny was put down. A few months later, when it became apparent that the clarification of the concept of "due obedience" would not be forthcoming from the courts, and the restlessness kept spreading to loyal sectors of the armed forces, we decided to pass the so-called Law of Due Obedience (*de Debida*[20]), by which Congress reestablished the limits to the prosecutions envisioned in our original project. We sought a point of convergence between the requirements of justice and prudence when confronted by a state of necessity, and this law helped us overcome the successive rebellions of Monte Caseros and Villa Martelli.

The people who opposed our policy, and criticized our initiatives to limit the trials, argue from the standpoint of a retributive conception of punishment according to which it is a duty to punish for every crime, and if one fails to do so, that failure cannot be compensated by any other social benefit. We believed, on the contrary, that the retributive conception of punishment is difficult to justify and square with the principles of social morality because punitive practices are justified only insofar as they are effective in preventing worse evils. Ultimately punishment is an instrument to develop the collective moral conscience, and it is neither the only instrument for that purpose nor the most important one. The revelation of the truth about past events, an impartial trial, and a moral sanction serve as much as or more than punishment to teach what are the limits of behaviors that a society is willing to accept.

Our defense of human rights went further than the trials of the commanders in chief of the armed forces and the terrorist chieftains who were responsible for the violations of human rights. We repealed discriminatory penal norms that imposed excessive sanction for political crimes, established the possibility of freedom for people undergoing due process, broadened the scope of conditional sanctions, limited the consequences of repeated offenses, diminished sanctions that were considered excessive and cruel, and bestowed the right, to those sentenced by military tribunals, to annul their sentence through a habeas corpus. One law established the same penalty for torture as for homicide, another punished those who knew of torture or homicide in military establishments or in police stations but did not denounce these crimes to the courts. Another law gave the same rights to children whether born in or out of wedlock, and we repealed a law which permitted the deprivation of a citizen of his nationality. We sent to Congress a legislative proposal which recognized the right of a conscientious objector with respect to military service. Argentina ratified the International Convention on Economic, Social, and Cultural Rights and the Inter-American Convention on Human Rights.

We successfully reconstructed the judiciary system, one of the most difficult and important tasks of the transition. For decades Argentine judicial practice had ignored basic Constitutional norms. The justice system, appealing to capricious interpretative constructs, had acquiesced in electoral fraud, *coups d'état*, the violation of human rights, the abuse of presidential powers and the state of siege, administrative corruption, and even Constitutional reform by military decree. I believe that with all these reforms and the trials of both the Junta commanders and the terrorists, during my government we set a firm foundation in Argentina for the rule of law, which is an essential component of democracy, one that had been missing in our country.

A NEW TRANSITION

When I handed over the government to my democratically elected successor, Carlos Menem (the victorious presidential candidate of the main opposition party), it could be said that Argentina had successfully carried out its transition from dictatorship to democracy. The rule of law had been reestablished and a change begun in our political culture that will help to consolidate democracy well into our future. I am proud of this achievement and many others. But our government did fail to transform the country's economic structures in its attempt to bring about sustained economic growth; also, our effort to promote a welfare state did not work and is in danger of being discredited by the economic collapse that came at the end of my government.

One reason that explains this failure is that we did not achieve a fundamental understanding among all actors in Argentina's transition to democracy. I am speaking of a broad understanding involving not only political protagonists but also social and economic actors. On one hand, the lingering political intolerance made it impossible to achieve such an understanding; on the other hand, our imagination failed us in our attempts to achieve this goal. But it is not a question of assigning blame. The fact remains that in one of its most difficult moments in history Argentina was left economically and financially isolated on the international scene, and our government was also isolated and unable to reach an agreement with the opposition on basic domestic policies.

I believe the reason we failed is ultimately that the competition for power, though now bridled by the rule of law, is still overwhelming, and makes the compromises and agreements that are an integral part of the democratic processes very difficult to come by. In this sense we are still in a transition to democracy.

After our party lost the presidential elections,[21] my resignation was demanded six months before the end of my mandate.[22] The economy was in disarray, there was hyperinflation, and on the social front there were conspiracies to take over the supermarkets. Though I yearned to fulfill my mandate and hand over the symbols of the presidency to Carlos Menem on the date established by the Constitution, I accepted the demand that I step down because I believed my resignation would protect the transition and better conserve and strengthen the democratic process, which at that moment seemed endangered.[23]

The government that followed my administration, after a period of trial and error, put in place a technically efficient and conservative economic team that has successfully encouraged a capitalism that rewards production and provides enormous profits to some sectors of society, while leaving millions by the wayside, accentuating the division between the rich and the poor and creating a dual society of the haves and have-nots. With respect to the privatization of the economy this team has carried out many policies that the country needed, and others that we initiated but could not carry out because we were blocked by the opposition. But this economic team keeps afloat on top of a gerrymandered political structure constituted of rival and opposed interest groups. It is not based on a social or political consensus or understanding that we should be trying to achieve. Meanwhile the justice system and Congress have been overridden and undermined, a process facilitating corruption and providing a poor example of democracy in action.

The defense of democracy in our country requires the concerted action of those who are willing to defend it, and who have sufficient maturity to delay the discussion of the finer points of ideological differences to find common ground upon which to continue building democracy. The agenda of a new coalition committed to democracy must rescue the public domain, consolidate the rule of law by means of the institutions of representative democracy, reaffirm national sovereignty, reconstruct the social welfare state, and create the instruments to regulate markets to oppose monopolies and to implement industrial and export policies. This does not mean that we should undo those transformations of the economy brought about by the current government that the country needs and which we initiated. On the contrary, we must achieve an understanding that will permit these transformations to serve the majority of the people and not the few.

ONE MORE STEP: CONSTITUTIONAL REFORM

When I was president of Argentina, I created a bipartisan council, *El Consejo para la Consolidation de la Democracia*, in 1985 to study the need to reform the Constitution. The Council reached the conclusion that a constitutional reform was necessary to decentralize the powers concentrated in the executive branch of government. My successor also wanted to reform the Constitution to remove a constitutional restraint that prohibited a president from succeeding himself in office. During the first years of the Menem administration, I opposed this excessively narrow view of constitutional reform. But I was also uncertain whether a divided opposition would be able to stop the president from lifting the constitutional restraint to his reelection by means of a plebiscite. The government was considering a plebiscite to enforce its view on constitutional reform—an initiative that would have bitterly divided the country and weakened the respect for democracy in Argentina.

In the light of these circumstances and as president of my party, the Union Civica Radical, an agreement was negotiated with representatives of the Menem administration on the articles of constitutional reform our parties could support. On the one hand, our party agreed to support the right of the president to be reelected to a second term, though not to a third term, while shortening the presidential term from six to four years. On the other hand, the government agreed to a series of constitutional reforms to limit the powers of the executive while strengthening the legislature, the judiciary, and the representation of the opposition in government.

In 1994 a Constitutional Assembly was elected. After weeks of deliberations a Constitution was approved that included these reforms and others. Finally our national authorities swore their allegiance to the newly reformed Constitution.

The new Constitution, besides permitting the reelection of the president for a second term, strengthens guarantees for human rights by incorporating international human rights treaties into its text. It also creates the position of Prime Minister, answerable to Congress; it establishes the election of the mayor of the country's largest city, Buenos Aires (the mayor was previously designated by the President), it determines that senators will be elected directly by the people and not designated by provincial legislatures; it establishes that provinces will be represented by two senators from the majority and one from the minority to assure the representation of the opposition in the Senate; and it also establishes a run off system for presidential elections and creates an independent judiciary review board.

The end result of this process is that for the first time since 1853 the country has a Constitution backed by all sectors of society and imposed by none. It is a Constitution that protects the rights of all our citizens, limits the executive branch of government, and strengthens the representation of the opposition. In May 1995 Argentina held its third consecutive national election. President Menem was reelected and the country headed into its third consecutive democratic administration with an open and strengthened democratic institutional structure whose legitimacy is unquestioned. I believe the constitutional reform of 1994 carried the transition to democracy in Argentina one step further.

NOTES

1. A mind-set developed which fueled border rivalries and the Malvinas-Falklands War; a similar mind-set may be behind the nationalist struggles in the countries of Eastern Europe that were under communist dictatorships.

2. Raúl Alfonsín was elected on October 29, 1983, and inaugurated on December 10 that same year. As presidential candidate of the Unión Cívica Radical he obtained more than 50 percent of the vote, defeating for the first time the labor-based Peronist Party.

3. More than ten thousand persons "disappeared" during the military government, and more than one thousand people were killed by terrorists between 1973 and 1980. During that particularly brutal period of our history (1976–1982) international border tensions with Chile almost led to war, and Argentina lost a war with the United Kingdom over the Malvinas (Falkland Islands).

4. An account of the kind of modernization that goes hand in hand with the authoritarian mind-set is found in Guillermo A. O'Donnell, *Modernization and Bureaucratic-Authoritarianism* (Berkeley, Calif.: Institute of International Studies, 1973).

5. See A. James Gregor, *Italian Fascism and Developmental Dictatorship* (Princeton, N.J.: Princeton University Press, 1979).

6. Amitai Etzioni, *The Moral Dimension: Towards a New Economics* (New York: The Free Press, 1988). Etzioni presents cogent arguments for the development of the public dimension of society.

7. For example, in Argentina those efforts to "prepare" the country for democracy in the 1930s, 1940s, 1950s, 1960s, and 1970s by the military-civilian dictatorships were failures.

8. Alejandro Díaz writes at the beginning of his *Essays on the Economic History of the Argentine Republic* (New Haven, Conn.: Yale University Press, 1970), 1, "It is common now-a-days to lump the Argentine economy with the economies of other Latin American nations. Some opinion puts it among such less developed nations as India and Nigeria. Yet, most economists writing during the first three decades of this century would have placed Argentina among the advanced countries . . ."

9. Robert A. Potash in his work *The Army and Politics in Argentina (1928–1945)* (Stanford, Calif.: Stanford University Press, 1969), 55–56, describes the civilian component of the government that arose from the coup of September 6, 1930, the first in the series of coups mentioned above.

10. It is the obstacle faced by the new democracies in the territories of the ex–Soviet Union and in Eastern Europe.

11. See Nunca Más (The Report of the National Commission on the Disappearance of Persons) (New York: Farrar, Straus, Giroux, 1986).

12. See Presidential Decrees 157 and 158, December 13, 1983.

13. The National Commission on the Disappearance of Persons (Comisión Nacional sobre la Desparición de Personas).

14. The military junta, before handing over the government, enacted the "Law of National Pacification," which granted immunity from prosecution to suspected terrorists and all members of the armed forces (Law No. 22924, September 22, 1983).

15. Law No. 23040, December 27, 1983.

16. Separate trials were held for the leaders of terrorist organizations, some of whom were extradited from foreign countries to stand trial.

17. See Article 11 of Law 23049, which modified the Code of Military Justice and was passed by Congress February 14, 1984.

18. Law 23492 promulgated on December 24, 1986, known as "la Ley del Punto Final" (the Law of the Full Stop).

19. See *The New York Times*, April 18, 1987, 1.

20. Law 23251, June, 4 1987.

21. May 12, 1989.

22. Alfonsín was elected for a six-year term on December 10, 1989.

23. Alfonsín resigned on July 8, 1989, and Carlos Menem was inaugurated president six months ahead of schedule.

Chapter 3

The Rise of Public Legitimation in the Soviet Union and Eastern Europe

DANIEL N. NELSON

INTRODUCTION

Eastern Europe's communist regimes appeared suddenly to collapse in 1989 while, at the same time, ethno-nationalism, labor strife, and other conditions were leading the USSR toward internal chaos. These circumstances lent themselves to the inference that Marxist-Leninist regimes had all suffered from an explosion of pent-up resentment and disillusionment. Such a pressure-cooker image suggests that new governments are the products of revolutions that broke entirely from past political trends.

My thesis here is quite different. Instead of revolutions in 1989, I see the transformation of political life in Eastern Europe and the USSR to have been much more incremental. In the following chapter, I discuss a movement over ten to twenty years toward public legitimation of political authority that, in the process, rid these countries of communist party regimes.

This process, now largely historical, nevertheless forms a basis from which new political parties and their leaders must arise. It is a process of democratization that, while having completed one phase, continues as the difficult task of re-legitimation is undertaken by politicians in a plural and competitive environment. Popular expectations, overt in the waning years and even months of communist rule, cannot now be assuaged with the kind of rhetoric and simulated change practiced for two generations by Leninist party elites.

Prior to Mikhail Gorbachev's leadership in the USSR, it commonly was assumed that ruling elites in communist states made policy with little or no regard for the opinions or preferences of the people they ruled. Mass public opinion and even specific groups within that public were thought to have no input into the formation of policies or, ultimately, authoritative decision. T. H. Rigby, for example, wrote about the Soviet case as late as 1980 that

One arena which is typically of great if not decisive importance in Western policy-formation, namely the public political arena, is almost empty in the Soviet case. And the confrontation of ends . . . is as a rule deeply concealed and disguised, and the debate is about *means*. In [the West], policy-making has rather the character of a rough spectator sport, with much mutual abuse between the umpire, players and their supporters; in the [USSR], it is a *task* like any other.[1]

Rigby did acknowledge that the public political arena was "not entirely empty" in cases such as environmental issues, and that Polish events (i.e., those of 1980 and earlier) had reminded communist leaders that there were probably limits "beyond which it may be unsafe to push the masses, and thereby a probable influence in policy." In large part, however, what the public thought and preferred had nothing to do with the political arena. Unless populations engaged in mass protest as in Poland, communist parties in power were thought to ignore popular opinions or desires.

In a preliminary study about the relationship between public opinion and public policy in communist states, I used data from the late 1970s in Poland, Czechoslovakia, and Hungary to investigate the degree of "congruence" between opinion and policy.[2] Although data were imprecise and the time span limited, it appeared that substantial shifts of opinion toward negative evaluations and expectations of systemic performance had occurred about the same time as increased fluctuation in socioeconomic and military expenditures. Further, these changes corresponded roughly in terms of their magnitude (that is, sizeable changes in opinion paralleled large shifts in expenditures). Such a preliminary look at these data did not resolve the issue, but instead implied that the assumed absence of a link between public opinion and public policy in communist states of that period deserved more exploration.

By 1989, my earlier observations were overtaken by events. In the USSR and even more so in Eastern European states, communist rule succumbed to mass antipathy. Systemic performance, leadership competence, and administrative credibility were criteria on which communist party regimes were judged and failed. Central planning agencies, secret police, and the Party's *nomenklatura* have not vanished entirely, and reform will be slowed by institutional recalcitrance. But, in Europe's eastern half, there will be no turning back from systems based on responsiveness.

This chapter concerns the effects of a widened "public political arena" that first transformed elite-mass relations in communist states, contributed to their collapse, and now determines the prospects for a transition to stable democracy.

THE EMERGENCE OF PUBLIC LEGITIMACY: GENERAL CONSIDERATIONS

The legitimation of communist regimes was asserted on the basis of alleged historical inevitability (the dialectical materialism of Marx) and the vanguard status that Leninist parties arrogated unto themselves. A dictatorship of the proletariat, sanctioned by Marx as "the necessary transit point to the abolition of class distinctions generally,"[3] was used to rationalize the party's unswerving leadership and guidance in the building of communism. The proletarian class dictatorship was the ideological justification for the party's rigid centralism and its authoritarian policies from Lenin and Stalin through the first fifteen years of Eastern European communist regimes.

During Khrushchev's tenure, at the CPSU's Twenty-second Congress, the "all-people's state" replaced the proletarian dictatorship as the accepted self-description of ruling communist states. The relationship between rulers and ruled did not, however, change in structure or substance throughout what was then the Warsaw Pact region. The public political arena remained largely uninhabitable during the 1950s and 1960s, not only because the Soviets and domestic Stalinists used coercion. Extensive growth produced industrial recovery that also gave the appearance of positive performance, while a variety of leadership strategies enabled Eastern European and Soviet leaders to mix various appeals to win a modicum of public acquiescence and acceptance. Structures, processes, and policies generally were not debated in the public realm because the party and its elite understood the limits of Soviet tolerance, and because their own precarious positions demanded that they maintain an aura of infallibility.

But this mode of legitimation never worked well, and the diminishing effectiveness of ideologically based legitimacy became painfully evident in the 1970s as the end of extensive growth and development was reached in the USSR and Eastern Europe.[4] Although the data indicating a decline in economic expansion within communist Europe are relatively clear, their explanation is not. It is, however, at least certain that several factors contributed to a decline in growth including

growing labor scarcity, higher costs of energy and raw materials, increasing consumer expectations for a higher level of living that suggest trade-offs favoring consumption over investment, a growing burden of foreign indebtedness, and systemic factors that dampen initiative, innovation, and willingness on the part of the population to strive for higher quality and greater productivity.[5]

This assessment by Thad Alton was more warranted in some prerevolutionary countries of communist Europe than others. Yet, despite variations, it is generally true that popular expectations and workforce disenchantment, coupled with many structural factors, contributed to the economic slowdown of the USSR and Eastern Europe. The linkage between mass support and policy was already evident in the late 1970s, when, as diminished "willingness . . . to strive" and heightened expectations combined to form a substantial obstacle to the performance of centrally planned socialist (state socialist) economies. The public arena was beginning to widen.

In the late 1970s Eastern Europeans of all strata and segments outside the *nomenklatura* began to withdraw their tacit acceptance of the party's justification for central planning and sociopolitical controls in the face of widespread evidence of state socialism's poor performance. Exceptions to this aggregate portrait—most notably, the public acceptance of Kadarism at that time—have subsequently proved to be transient. One may point out, certainly, that East Germans in 1953, Hungarians in 1956, and Poles in 1956, 1968, and 1970 had, much earlier, evinced their willingness to oppose the Communist Party at any cost. But, in the late 1970s, we see more than the courageous but futile violent outbursts against communist rule. There was, instead, the development of mass disaffection incorporating even those who had remained pliant before.[6]

By the 1980s, party leaders' admonitions to sacrifice for future benefits and for vaguely defined internationalist goals, halfheartedly believed in prior decades, fell on deaf ears. Some leaders, to be sure, continued to make the same old appeals.[7] But, as Soviet Academician Abel Aganbegyan has said, "The workers in the first place are interested in a better life."[8] People, in fact, demanded through their attitudinal antagonism, behavioral indifference, and occasional protest or strike, a turn toward intensive growth, and new standards for performance, that is, an environment where bigger is not necessarily better. Instead, there was a yearning for a qualitatively better life, where opportunities were not allocated from Gosplan or Gosbank, and where a civil society could emerge from beneath the heavy weight of party and state bureaucracy.

The workforce, in particular, may not have fully understood how such a new ethos would affect the individual employee, for example, by having income tied to productivity, promotion linked to merit, and subsidized services and commodities rising steeply in cost. Prior to 1989, worker disaffection had not led to mass unrest. Communist authorities, excluding only Romania and Albania, had been forced to acknowledge these demands and preferences. Desperate to establish a new equilibrium, such regimes even expressed cautious willingness to work with "minority views" or organizations reflecting public interests. In cases such as Hungary, however, the demise in short order (roughly 1986–1988) of a "Kadarist consensus" meant that the authorities could not afford caution, and began to accept criticism of the political system itself from opposition groups.[9] For Poland, of course, Jaruzelski had known since 1980–1981 that the opposition commanded the allegiance of the vast majority of Poles.

Substantively different elite-mass relations in communist Europe, then, began to be exhibited in the 1980s. To have a society and an economy acknowledged as distinct—and legitimately so—from the party's suzerainty had been a goal of reformers, Marxist or not, in Eastern Europe and the USSR. To the degree that such a goal was achieved even before 1989, political life moved outside the party and its *nomenklatura*, as competition and conflict over resources inherent to politics were undertaken elsewhere.

The next logical step was institutionalized political pluralism, connoting the demise of the party's leading role. Such pluralism was not a foregone conclusion everywhere in communist Europe, was opposed by many, and might have been derailed by rampant strikes, demonstrations, or ethnic unrest. Nevertheless, the discussion of such possibilities became acceptable by the late 1980s in some countries, and less fraught with risk in all but Romania. In Poland and the USSR, genuine pluralism—where expression of diverse preferences engenders new political organizations—developed rapidly, with Soviet elections in March 1989 and Polish elections of June 1989 being catalysts for reactivated liberal, conservative, peasant, and nationalist organizations. Hungarians moved even more rapidly, creating and re-creating political parties to the left and right in 1988 and 1989 well before elections were even announced.

The question of legitimacy thus became public *before* the demise of communist regimes. This qualitative transformation of elite-mass relations did not occur everywhere at once, having been more latent in the case of Romania, and most advanced in Poland, Hungary, and the USSR. Elsewhere, however, communist states jettisoned to a greater or lesser degree their role as a distant vanguard, and began the process—distasteful to older party members—of seeking public favor. With Poland and Hungary as the paramount examples, communist elites began to recognize the requirement of public trust. They were painfully aware that they did not have that trust, and thus had no way to deal with the endemic problems that had fostered mass disaffection in the first place.

Perestroika, glasnost, and *demokratizatsiya* were Mikhail Gorbachev's responses to the Soviet Union's economic demise and sociopolitical malaise. They were, in fact, vague political expressions that subsumed a myriad of policy adaptations necessitated, in Gorbachev's view, by performance failure. Taken together, however, they had the intent of undoing much of central planning while imposing upon Soviet society the ethos of competitiveness and merit. Certainly not the product of leaders' own musings about the ideal Soviet society, *perestroika* and the other guiding concepts were means by which Gorbachev and his allies sought to preempt what they saw as dangerous signals of mass instability in the USSR if little or nothing was done. Indeed, it was Gorbachev's erstwhile ally, Boris Yeltsin, who warned at the Twenty-seventh Party Congress in March 1986 that the stability of the Soviet Union could not be taken for granted. Now, in the aftermath of nationality unrest from the Baltic to the Caucasus and Central Asia, Yeltsin's words seem prophetic. One must acknowledge that either the pace of change was too little and too late *or* that the tensions had long ago become severe and political change offered an opportunity for such issues to rise to the surface.

That ruling communist parties tried, in their waning years, to become more responsive must be put into proper perspective. This striving for a public legitimacy based upon systemic responsiveness to mass preferences and upon systemic performance in light of those public needs and demands did not indicate a revived sense of public trust. Instead, it was a clear symptom that Leninist parties were incapacitated. Political cultures of communist states in Eastern Europe were transformed from conditions in which leaders acted as autocrats and oligarchs into ones in which expertise and a populist flair became required leadership characteristics.[10] But it was not enough to obtain a broadly based popular trust.

Political culture, "a particular distribution of political attitudes, values, feelings, information and skills,"[11] embodies subjective orientations between rulers and ruled. Years ago, Almond and Verba distinguished among parochial, subject, and participatory political cultures.[12] None of these archetypical patterns of elite-mass relations exists in a pure form, but the changing mix of political cultures is evident and the causes and consequences of such a transformation are observable. As the Soviet Union and Eastern Europe experienced the incremental emergence of a participatory mass political culture, citizenship *qua* "subject" was no longer accepted, and old appeals and leadership stratagems were inadequate alone to ensure willing obedience. Implicit to this cultural shift was an expansion of the "public political sphere" affecting policy formulation, enactment, and implementation and the stratum of political elites itself.

But what effects are these? How does a more participatory political environment influence policy? These questions have, of course, theoretical importance for all systems in transition from authoritarian systems to plural, competitive environments.

Lowell Dittmer, in his essay "Comparative Communist Political Culture," distinguished independent, dependent, and intervening roles of political culture.[13] Dittmer argued that political culture, both in its "official code" (ideological beliefs) and "traditional code" (history, religion, etc.), affected political actors and institutions. On the other hand, variation in political culture was induced by "low visibility, diurnal events" such as modernization or "epochal events" such as wars or economic crashes.[14] Finally, political culture can play an intermediary role in that politicians "find it necessary to employ the symbolic resources of the existing political culture" to put their policies into effect.[15]

With some modifications, Dittmer's view—that political culture cannot be seen simply as cause or effect—is useful today for postcommunist conditions. We should add to official and traditional "codes" in political culture a "popular code," composed of nonideological and nontraditional values such as consumerism, pluralism, and any number of modern, secular values. This notion of a "popular code" embedded within political culture is particularly clear in the postcommunist circumstances of Eastern European and post-Soviet systems.

With such an addition, the Dittmer formulation helps to underscore the importance of changes prior to 1989 that brought legitimation into the public political arena. With legitimation becoming a more public process even while communist systems still held power, we should have seen evidence that the "popular code" element of political culture became increasingly influential in the allocation of resources in these systems. Simultaneously, of course, the distribution of attitudes, values, and other component orientations of political culture were increasingly affected by regime policies.

Almond and Powell correctly expected reciprocal linkages between public attitudes and policies. Citizens of all political systems, they wrote, have attitudes about system, process, and policy.[16] Concerning policy, citizens (and leaders) have certain expectations of government, namely, the goals of policy and the means by which they are to be achieved.[17] On the other side of the coin, a government's survivability will, because of its effectiveness in making and implementing policy, be heightened when its legitimacy is more secure,[18] and will try to inculcate positive, supportive, and obedient attitudes and values—that is, to affect the distribution of subjective orientations comprising a political culture.

These relationships, I submit, were increasingly present in Europe's communist party states of the 1980s and before; mass subjective orientations, and the key to legitimation that they held, were linked to the tenure of those who made and implemented policy as well as to the formulation, selections, and implementation of policies themselves. They—public attitudes and preferences—eventually led to the collapse of policy and leadership in communist Europe. But how were these changes evident? What were the new subjective orientations of the populations that resisted regime efforts both to socialize citizens and to intimidate them if alternative values were expressed? A closer examination of Soviet and Eastern European circumstances in the 1980s, leading up to 1989, can shed light on this backdrop to fundamental shifts in the region's political life.

THE GROWTH OF THE PUBLIC POLITICAL ARENA IN THE USSR

In the Soviet case, we do not have the advantage of consistent survey research with which to gauge changing levels of attitudinal support for policies, institutions, or personages of the CPSU over a lengthy period. Prior to the mid-1980s, surveys within the USSR were limited in scope, and provided few methodological specifics by which to judge reliability or validity of findings.[19] Exceptions to this rule were occasional studies of workers that evinced greater sophistication and care[20] and some of the work by Boris Grushin's Institute of Public Opinion at *Komsomolskaya Pravda*. Yet, there is unmistakable evidence that discussion of public concerns and preferences was a central feature of formulating specific policy components of *perestroika*, and the principal rationale for public criticisms embodied in the concept of *glasnost*.

When Mikhail Gorbachev began speaking of the "fight for *perestroika*," he invariably stressed the requirement of popular support. At the February 1988 CPSU Central Committee Plenum, Gorbachev noted that

for the first time in many decades we really feel the socialist pluralism of views. This is something uncommon, and it is being assessed in different ways; it demands study, analysis and elucidation. Behind all that we must see the principal thing— growing support for the policy of restructuring on the part of the people.[21]

Socialist pluralism quickly became the substantive core of both *glasnost* and *demokratizatsiya*. Whether in media and public fora, *or* in party and state procedures, incorporating a diversity of views was at the core of Gorbachev's vision—albeit, he hoped and intended, a diversity within vaguely defined boundaries. Without socialist pluralism, Gorbachev seems to have said, the public support for *perestroika* could not be generated and/or maintained.

Less than two months after his speech at the Central Committee Plenum, Gorbachev was in the Uzbek capital of Tashkent, primarily to meet with Afghan communist leader, Najibullah. In Tashkent, however, the general secretary spoke before a meeting of the Uzbek Republic party leaders, and that speech was carried on all-union television the night of April 9, 1988. In that speech, according to Radio Liberty, Gorbachev spoke of "one important victory" achieved by *perestroika*—namely, it had "set the whole mass of the people in motion."[22]

Later, in an interview with reporters in Moscow on March 4, 1990, Gorbachev emphasized the indispensable role of the people in fostering *perestroika*. The general secretary stated that "[we] all need *perestroika*. This is the actual basis for unity. The time now is such that we simply must, we have to listen to and understand one another . . . simply because every- thing depends on us! Unless we change, nothing else will change. Man is the key element."[23]

Abel Aganbegyan, economist and member of the Soviet Academy, often referred to as the architect of *perestroika*, specified that any reforms, including price increases, had to be carefully linked to "what the people decide." Although Aganbegyan did not imply a plebescite on every aspect or stage of *perestroika*, he expressed the obvious dependence of the Gor- bachev program upon popular acceptance. Gorbachev underscored the need to end irrational prices, while assuring that a full public discussion would be held prior to any changes and that anyone who lost (in terms of living standards) due to price revisions would be compensated from public funds.[24]

Radical exponents of reform agreed with Gorbachev on the issue of public support. Economist Nikolai Shmelev, who made a name for himself during 1987 and 1988 with articles in principal Soviet journals (especially in *Novyi Mir*) criticizing the misplaced emphasis, slow progress, and limited effectiveness of Gorbachev's programs, underscored the necessity of mass support.[25] By mid-1988, Shmelev was arguing that the public was nervous and afraid,[26] and unlikely to regard restructuring as having produced any benefit—prophetic given the further economic decline in subsequent years.

The same tie between policies of reform, mass support, and regime legitimacy is suggested by the comments of one of America's most experienced observers of the USSR, George F. Kennan. Kennan wrote, in The *New York Review of Books*, that "the Soviet economy cannot be made to function as it should. . .until there can be implanted in . . . workers, foremen and administrators . . . [an] 'inner stimuli.'"[27] Such stimuli, it is clear, depend on the substantive content of *glasnost* and *demokratizatsiya*, the latter implying "a greater measure of consultation, of the feelings and views of people at the bottom."[28] Jerry Hough echoed these assessments when he argued that "any really substantial reform . . . does not depend solely on a general secretary's consolidation of power in the Politburo and the Central Committee." He [Gorbachev] must, Hough continued,

persuade ordinary officials to work with a sense of enthusiasm and professionalism; he must persuade students and young intellectuals not to go into the streets in a large-scale and threatening way; he must persuade workers not to riot in the face of higher prices, greater discipline, and demands for other sacrifices. He must accomplish this with respect to both Russians and non-Russians, whose interests and demands can be quite contradictory.[29]

Hough may have been reflecting on an appeal that the Central Committee did, in fact, make in May 1987 calling for the Soviet people to exhibit responsibility for "the fate of socialism" while appealing to "the labor ethic, to the professional pride of working people, to the patriotism of the Soviet people."[30] By 1990, of course, CPSU appeals were falling on deaf ears.

Efforts to engender mass approval for Gorbachev and his policies took on many forms. The general secretary's own speeches and appearances became, by 1987, an omnipresent feature of Soviet television, and he "appeared on television more often than any Soviet leader has previously done, even exceeding his own past record."[31] Recognizing that broadcast media were the principal means by which to communicate with the Soviet masses, Gorbachev took his message to the airwaves with increasing urgency and, in his late June 1989 appeal to end nationalities' unrest, genuine poignancy.

We also saw a wide and rapid expansion of the media's investigatory role, ferreting out waste, inefficiency, and corruption. Of particular note was the introduction of "Prozhektor perestroiki" on Soviet television. This program, as the name implies, was intended to shed light on the progress, or lack thereof, of *perestroika* in economic and governmental bureaucracy. Reporting on this program, a Radio Liberty researcher noted its utility as "a barometer of public opinion" by "making those responsible answer criticisms."[32]

An additional acknowledgement of the need to tap public opinion was the creation, in early 1988, of the Center for Study of Public Opinion at the all-union level, directed by prominent Gorbachev supporter Tatyana Zaslavskaya. The mere establishment of such an institution was very significant. With explicit approval from a Politburo resolution, the Center began branches throughout the Soviet Union, central offices and computer facilities in Moscow, and adopted an independent status. Nominally, Zaslavskaya's new research team operated under the Central Council of Trade Unions, as opposed to working within the structure of the Academy of Sciences or the CPSU itself, which augured well for the Center's autonomy. That the Center began to publish a quarterly journal, *Mneniya*, suggested further an ability to report *publicly* findings on survey research.[33]

By late 1989 and 1990, polling had become a common activity in the USSR, inquiring about public attitudes on political, environmental, and sociological issues. The CPSU Central Committee Academy of Social Sciences Sociological Survey Center conducted a poll in late May and early June of 1989 to ascertain the political orientation of the population. They conducted the poll in eighteen regions of the country and received responses from just under 1,500 people.[34] In June of 1990, the USSR Academy of Sciences, jointly with the Sociological Center of the University of Houston, conducted a poll on environmental issues. Ninety-eight percent of all polled stated they were more concerned about the environment than growth in the crime rate, food shortages, the AIDS epidemic, and interethnic conflicts.[35]

One of the clearest indications of the increase in concern of public attitudes on current issues was revealed by a public opinion poll conducted by the USSR State Committee for Statistics. This poll differed dramatically from previous ones by virtue of its scale—101,000 workers, employees, *kolkhoz* members, and pensioners in all republics' *krays* and *oblasts* were polled on the subject of cooperative and individual labor activity.[36]

Even the KGB began, in the spring of 1988, to publish a column in the weekly *Argumenty i Fakty*, trying to present the intelligence/secret police establishment of the USSR in a positive light. By making such an overture to public opinion, it is clear that the KGB felt compelled to engage in public politics uncharacteristic of its past, save for the first years of the Bolshevik regime under Lenin. In reporting on this development, Viktor Yasmann of Radio Liberty observed that this step was meant to "promote the notion that the KGB is just another state organization that obeys the law, carries out its proper functions *and respects public opinion*."[37] After the September 30, 1988, shake-up that sent Chebrikov to head a Central Committee commission, the new KGB chief, Kryuchkov, accelerated the public image campaign, allowing a Moscow newspaper to visit and photograph central KGB offices and facilities, while himself meeting the press. Surely, Kryuchkov would not have entered the sphere of public politics or sought to make his organization appear as a "responsible and responsive state organization" unless public legitimation had by then become a presence within the Soviet polity too large to ignore.

From the statements of Gorbachev and those to his "left," from media programming, from the formation of new all-union sociological research institutes, and from the actions of principal regime institutions such as the KGB, then, there was substantial evidence that the regime quickly learned that *perestroika* would sink or swim on the basis of mass support. It—the Gorbachev regime and his policies—had to be seen as legitimate by far more than the stratum of intellectuals who appeared to have been his "natural constituency" in the first years of his rule.

All of the steps taken by Gorbachev to evince concern for public opinion and to foster criticisms of the bureaucracy while encouraging journalistic openness, were, of course, simultaneously an effort to mold that opinion. That is, the concern for public preferences was fashioned in order to foster public support and to mobilize the Soviet citizenry through the appearance that mass opinion had become germane, not to listen to complaints per se. In that sense, Gorbachev's talk of socialist pluralism certainly did not sanction the *creation* of diverse opinions, but rather recognized that it existed. S. Frederic Starr has said much the same when he wrote in 1988 that "Gorbachev is not creating change so much as uncorking it."[38]

Much of the developing pluralism in Soviet public opinion was demonstrated through the multiplicity of independent journals and their sponsoring "informal" grassroots associations. Only a small proportion of the 100,000 informal groups by 1990 had publications, and most had little connection with politics. Yet, those groups with publications were those with an agenda linked to public policy. Nevertheless, many of the periodicals appeared regularly, and were disributed quite openly. Semilegal contacts among like-minded individuals "began in the 1950s with networks of underground jazz fans [and] spread in the 1970s to the sphere of public affairs."[39] Their multiplication and extension into printed media, however, did not reach epidemic proportions until the Gorbachev period. Efforts by the authorities to maintain some kind of hold on these groups—by holding out the "carrot" of material support if members agreed to legal status and accompanying restrictions[40] and by allowing a national conference of such groups in Moscow during August 1987—did little or nothing to constrain the burgeoning pluralism. S. Frederic Starr observed, for instance, that "as public opinion gained in strength, it grew in diversity."[41]

A policy-effective element of such autonomous networking among informal groups concerned the environment and nuclear energy. It can be argued that the environmental movement was the leading edge (much more so than literary or religious dissidents ever were) of an all-union, multinational opposition to the authorities and their established policies. In the Russian Republic, opposition to nuclear power was particularly evident in cities such as Krasnodar because of dangers from nuclear waste.[42] In the Ukraine, widespread public opposition to adding more reactors at Chernobyl after the 1986 disaster resulted in a May 1987 decision to halt construction.[43] This networking of people against further nuclear development continued in 1988–1990, with leading Ukrainian scientists expressing negative views about environmental effects and possible dangers from accidents.[44] Fears of pollution became apparent throughout the Soviet Union, and generated large protest demonstrations against new petrochemical enterprises even in less-developed areas such as Ufa, capital of Bashkir ASSR.[45] The Aral Sea, Volga River, and many other sites of grievous environmental damage became causes for political activism, usually tied implicitly to other issues.

Environmental and nuclear energy concerns were visible examples of many new and diverse issues aired publicly and cross-nationally within the USSR in the 1980s. The linkage between peace/antiwar groups and the environmental movement was, for instance, one of the more interesting ties among grassroots groups.[46] These, in turn, sometimes overlapped with a heterogeneous collection of vaguely Eurosocialist clubs that one observer labeled a "new left"—followers of Gramsci, nineteenth-century Utopians, and people moving in other directions.[47] Additional ties among informal groups extended to issues intertwined with nationalities; family planning, for example, received increasing opposition among Central Asian populations—opposition that was reported in mainstream journals such as the pro-Gorbachev *Ogonok*.[48] *Kommunist Tadzhikistana*, according to a Radio Liberty report, noted in early 1988 the spread of debate about family planning beyond scientists and professionals to "all strata of the population."[49]

The most pronounced example of public opposition to the authorities and mass cohesion was the movement for independence by the Baltic states. Although Gorbachev attempted, through economic pressure and displays of military force, to constrain the Baltic states, he was not successful. In fact, Gorbachev's tough stance actually incited the Baltic states to work more cohesively toward independence. According to *Soviet/East European Report, Radio Free Europe/Radio Liberty,* Liina Tommisson, an official in Estonia's economics ministry, told reporters on May 17, 1990, that when Moscow cut off supplies to Lithuania, Estonia decreased its exports to the Soviet Union. Tommisson stated that such an action allowed Estonia to be "better prepared [to survive] an economic blockage" from the Soviet Union, if one were imposed.[50]

Gorbachev's choice to equate the declarations of Estonia and Latvia with that of Lithuania had the effect of strengthening and bonding the three states together in their fight for independence if not instigating similar actions by other republics and regions in the USSR. Mykhailo Horyn, the chairman of the Ukrainian "Rukh," presciently stated in an interview published in the Warsaw newspaper *Rzeczpospolita* that "Moscow's harsh actions against the Baltic states will ultimately force the Ukraine to secede as well."[51]

In the Soviet case, then, one can assemble a variety of impressionistic evidence suggesting that leaders, critics, and Western observers thought the future of Gorbachev and his policies rested with mass allegiance, not only, or principally, with elite forbearance. Further, the socialist pluralism of which Mikhail Gorbachev spoke frequently was his way of acknowledging a phenomenon begun some time ago, but which was proliferating throughout Soviet society. Gorbachev did not make public legitimation secure and permanent for Russia or other Soviet successor states. There is strong evidence that Gorbachev's efforts were meant to channel processes of change toward a participatory culture with centrally pronounced forms of liberalization—*demokratizatsiya* and *glasnost*—having little impact on Soviet citizens outside the intelligentsia. Indeed, several years after Gorbachev came to power, the masses remained indifferent or doubtful about the effects of glasnost.[52]

Yet, public legitimacy seems to have achieved a hold in the Soviet polity because of the leadership's needs, legal and procedural changes in the system enabling the elections of 1989 and 1990 to take on a genuinely open flavor, and the efforts of some groups who spoke most loudly or effectively. Its consequence for policy, as noted above, was greatest in realms such as environmental issues, but it became linked to the "high politics" of peace/war, ideology, and nationalities policy.

THE GROWTH OF THE PUBLIC POLITICAL ARENA IN EASTERN EUROPE

Political cultures of the six Warsaw Treaty Organization (Warsaw Pact) members—"Eastern Europe" in the political sense of having been most closely tied to the USSR—exhibited different distributions of political attitudes, values, feelings, information, and skills even while Soviet hegemony was effective.[53] Well before 1989, even a cursory assessment of the region revealed that Poland and Hungary had become manifestly more open and public in their debates about leadership and policy matters than Czechoslovakia, Bulgaria, East Germany, or Romania, and that these latter four countries varied greatly in official and popular "codes" (recalling Dittmer's notion of political culture). After the 1989 demise of communist systems, different patterns emerged—for example, with democratization seemingly less impeded in the "Northern Tier" than in Romania and Bulgaria, where ethnic rivalries, military intervention, and residual party *nomenklatura* all clouded the picture.

Notwithstanding inherent differences of tradition, socioeconomic levels, and other factors which constitute this disparate region, some obvious political characteristics grouped these states for two generations. This leads us to ask whether or not the expansion of the "public political arena" became a generalizable trait across European states that were ruled by communist parties. To what degree were there similar periods of an expanding public political life that helped to prepare and accelerate these systems' transitions? Among these six states, one found common international memberships in (the Council for Mutual Economic Assistance) CMEA and the Warsaw Pact, high (although varying greatly) economic and military dependence on the USSR, and a political experience over four decades traceable to occupation by the Soviet Red Army during and after World War II. All had to adjust to new Soviet leadership in the late 1980s, and then experience the retreat of communist parties from their hold on state institutions, leaving few people trained in democratic governance. All faced dim economic prospects in the 1990s, and several have had to deal with extremely high external debt.

Finally, all must find new means by which to mobilize the populace and generate renewed economic performance.

In addition to these historical and structural similarities, the six Eastern European states must deal with uncertain public support. During a decade and a half (from the mid-1970s to 1989), communist rule turned people away from support of the system and from public life. To attract people back into a supportive involvement with parties and government is necessary and not easily accomplished. In Tables 1 and 2, data are reported for responses to a question ("How does socialism work out in practice in your country?") asked of Eastern Europeans traveling in the West during three periods— 1975/76, 1979/80, and 1984/85—by polling organizations employed by Radio Free Europe. Data in Table 1 are the percentage by which positive and negative answers to that question changed from one period to another; Table 2 ranks the five countries for which data are available by the size of the "negative shift" (drop in positive plus increase in negative responses) from period to period.

The services of private polling firms (Gallup International, Inc., etc.) were utilized during these years to conduct continuous sampling of Eastern European nationals while they were in Western Europe, thereby obtaining interview data from large numbers of citizens from Czechoslovakia, Hungary, Poland, Romania, and Bulgaria. Although these data are collected by professional pollsters, and there are large samples of nationals from the five countries (East Germans were not included), it is nevertheless true that one should not regard small distinctions as significant since the probability of some measurement error is high.[54] These data remain, however, the only longitudinal and cross-national attitudinal data from Eastern Europe during that time, replicating the same questions for citizens of all countries over a lengthy period.

From this source, an aggregate portrait emerges of East Europeans' attitudes toward the performance of waning communist party regimes. Among these five cases, only Bulgaria exhibited a growth in positive ("well" or "very well") responses—showing a "net" increase of 7 percent in such positive responses. The renewed communists in Bulgaria, now the Bulgarian Socialist Party (BSP), may owe their relatively good electoral showing to these decidedly different views of the system and its performance. All other cases were negative, with Poland's and Romania's net changes in positive evaluations being *decidedly* negative. All five cases exhibited a growth in negative response, with a very small increase (+1 percent) among the Hungarian sample. Romanian and Czechoslovak re-

Table 1

Trends in Eastern European Attitudes, 1975/76–1984/85: "How Does Socialism Work Out in Your Country?" (percentage change from 1975/76 to 1979/80 to 1984/85)

	Czechosl			Hungary			Poland			Romania			Bulgaria		
	1	2	Net*	1	2	Net	1	2	Net	1	2	Net	1	2	Net
Change Posit. a)	-4	+2	-2	-4	+1	-3	-7	-12	-19	+7	-24	-17	+2	+5	+7
Change Negat. b)	+15	+1	+16	+2	-1	+1	+14	+21	+35	-6	+25	+19	+9	-5	+4
Net Shift c)	-19	+1	-18	-6	+2	-4	-21	-33	-54	+13	-49	-36	-7	+10	+3
Change Undecided	-10	-4	-14	+2	-2	0	-7	-9	-16	-1	-3	-4	-11	0	-11

Source: Author's adaptation of data reported in *Radio Free Europe Area Audience and Opinion Research*, "Political Legitimacy in Eastern Europe: A Comparative Study" (March 1987), Table 6, p. 18.

*In column headed 1, percentages shown are differences between surveys conducted by *RFEAAOR* 1979/80 and those conducted in 1975/76. In column headed 2, percentages are differences between surveys conducted by *RFEAAOR* in 1984/85 and those conducted in 1979/80. The "Net" column is simply the addition of the two previous columns.

a) "Change Positive" is percentage difference of the country sample responding "very well" and "well" in Period 1 and Period 2, respectively.

b) "Change Negative" is percentage difference of the country sample responding "very badly" and "badly" in Period 1 and Period 2, respectively.

c) Net Shift is sum of change in positive and negative responses. For example, in Czechoslovakia in Period 1, one finds negative reponses to have increased by 15 percent, while positive declined by 4 percent. *Growth* in the percentage of negative responses and a decline in positive answers take the same sign (negative), and equal -19 percent. When positive responses grew and negative responses declined, e.g., Romania in Period 1, both changes take a positive sign and total +13 percent.

spondents also were far more critical, in that "badly" or "very badly" answers grew by 19 percent and 16 percent, respectively.

Combining the change in positive responses with the change in critical answers (with growth in negative evaluations taking the same negative sign as a decline in positive), one finds Poland and Romania to have had extremely large turnarounds in levels of public support, with Czechoslovakia showing a moderate loss of mass approval (net shift of -18 percent), while opinion change in Hungary (through 1985) was quite small, and

48 *After Authoritarianism*

Table 2
Change in "Net Shift" of Evaluations of Socialist Performance in Eastern Europe: A Comparison of Trends 1975/76–1984/85 (ranked by size of negative shift)

	Period 1 1975/76–1979/80	Period 2 1979/80–1984/85	Net
First (largest negative shift)	Poland	Romania	Poland
Second	Czechoslovakia	Poland	Romania
Third	Bulgaria	Czechoslovakia	Czechoslovakia
Fourth	Hungary	Hungary	Hungary
Fifth (least negative shift)	Romania	Bulgaria	Bulgaria

Source: See Table 1.

Note: Net Shift combines decline in positive responses with increase in negative responses or vice-versa. A decrease in positive responses and an increase in negative responses are both given negative signs; an increase in positive responses and a decline in negative answers are both regarded as positive signs. Author's tabulations from *RFEAAOR* data in Table 1, "Net Shift" row.

Bulgaria actually had a net shift toward a positive image of the regime's performance.

Most indicative of declining ambivalence about regime performance, and perhaps suggestive of the emergent extremism that has begun to crop up in the area's nascent democracies since 1990, is the tendency of fewer and fewer respondents to express indecision about the performance of socialism in their country. Poland and Czechoslovakia, in the 1975/76–1984/85 decade, saw an important drop in the "undecided" responses, with almost all of that new decisiveness clearly going toward negative evaluations.

These broad trends connote a shift in elite-mass relations so severe that none of the ruling communist parties in Eastern Europe had any hope of regaining the willing obedience of populations they governed. By June 1989, electoral data from Poland demonstrated an irrevocable loss—barring coercion that was impossible to impose—of political control for the Communist Party. Similarly, these data suggested that the Hungarian communists would become no more than one of the competitors in 1990, with prospects for a small proportion of the vote; in fact, the Hungarian "socialists" led by Pogzgay and others received only a tenth of the vote. The shift leading to such events combined several features, according to opinion data—generally a decline in positive assessments, with most of that decline contributing to a rise in negative evaluations. Simultaneously, a smaller and smaller proportion of Eastern European populations remained ambivalent, as issues of public policy and political leadership seem to have necessitated judgments about system performance.

While such a "silent revolution," to borrow Ronald Ingelhart's term, did not predict a date for the downfall of communist party regimes, it nevertheless provided a basis for creating alternative, "underground" societies in contradiction to the official environment in which the party's leading role was uncompromising.

Communist party regimes in Eastern Europe were long cognizant of their diminished public support and they made strenuous efforts to deflect public antipathy. Orchestrated reform such as Kadar's New Economic Mechanism of 1968, simulated change involving structural and procedural modification, and personnel shuffles *all* had long records in Eastern Europe. Self-management, self-government, and self-financing were all parts of earlier party-decreed responses to evidence of public disaffection.

By the mid-1980s, however, none of the halfway measures tried before had any residual momentum. Most economic measures during the 1980s induced only paltry growth or none at all, and other data suggested no way out of the malaise. Capital productivity (NMP [net material product] per fixed assets)—a key indicator of an economy's potential for recovery—changed predominantly in a negative direction for all Eastern European countries during the mid-to-late 1980s.[55] The self-proclaimed intention of the centrally planned economies of CMEA to accelerate "intensive" development,[56] accepted halfheartedly by party elites in the GDR, Bulgaria, and Czechoslovakia, and not at all by the Romanian dictator, Nicolae Ceausescu, would have been implemented only if there had been pressure to do so from below coupled with a willingness to live with immediate discomforts (higher prices, bankruptcy, and unemployment). Given the substantial disaffection in Eastern Europe by 1984/85, and the spread of discontent during 1985–1988 to Hungary, Bulgaria, East Germany, and Czechoslovakia as economies stagnated and the Soviet Union itself changed, such quiescent forbearance was impossible to obtain on behalf of regime-initiated reforms.

In Poland and Hungary the public political sphere became enlarged years before elsewhere in the region. It is not possible to identify a date when this process began, but we can certainly see evidence that leaders and their policies where topics of open, public debate in Poland for two decades.

Advances in survey research were made in Polish academic circles in the 1960s. Although findings were not often given to the masses, there was a recognition that the regimes of Gomulka and, after 1970, Gierek, had to concern themselves with levels of, and trends in, public support. That concern, of course, was not benign, and the authorities did not regard themselves as bearing some responsibility to elicit popular preferences and evaluations. Rather, they (especially in the Gierek years) wanted to nip trouble "in the bud" via a better knowledge of public opinion.

During Solidarity's first period of legal activity (1980–1981) the spread of survey research was very rapid, not only under the auspices of universities and Solidarity, but in the government itself. The Jaruzelski regime undertook regular soundings of public concerns and preferences through its Center for Social Opinion Research (CBOS, after the Center's initials in Polish), headed by Colonel Stanislaw Kwiatkowski. An older polling organization at Polish Radio and Television, the Center for Public Opinion Research (or OBOP, again from the Polish initials) also continued its operations. University, trade union, Solidarity, and other polling also went on. The national surveys of Poles (the *Polacy* studies) were undertaken by University of Warsaw social scientists, and represented the most thorough data-collection efforts in communist Europe.[57]

Not only did the Polish population evaluate the performance of the communist system in highly negative terms (see Table 1); Poles also *expected* to be able to articulate that disaffection—an expectation the regime had to learn to accept. When an official (CBOS) national poll of 1,300 people was conducted in November 1987, it pointed to an "overwhelmingly negative public mood" and to a substantial belief that there was a risk of a "serious explosion" in the coming year (1988). Although the entire contents of the report were not released to the public, state-controlled broadcast and print media did, in fact, report the survey's findings that 80 percent of Poles said the country's mood was uneasy, 80 percent had entirely negative opinions about the government, and 60 percent thought that there were reasons for "a serious explosion [and] open social conflict."[58]

Efforts by the PUWP (Polish United Workers Party) leadership to find ways to vent public disaffection in other ways were numerous. On January 1, 1988, for example, Poland became the first Eastern European state to establish an official ombudsman (referred to by Polish law as a civil rights spokesman). The ombudsman—at that time, Ewa Letowska—was, in short order, swamped by complaints of various kinds. Although an ombudsman in communist Poland could not alone cut through governmental obstacles to effect justice for citizens, the mere establishment of such a post in 1988 implied that the authorities were trying every means at their disposal to reduce social antagonism without relinquishing their political monopoly.[59]

Concern for its public legitimation was, thus, readily discernible in the actions of the PUWP government headed by Jaruzelski. The many other indicators of the regime's sensitivity to mass support require more detail than is possible here. Even before compromise with the opposition in early 1989, efforts to coexist with the Roman Catholic Church, an amnesty of political prisoners, the creation of PRON (the Patriotic Movement for National Rebirth) after martial law and later a "Consultative Council" to co-opt important opinion makers, and a necessarily tolerant approach toward Solidarity and the larger underground society—*all* reflected the much-enlarged public domain in which the Polish communist party regime tried to continue its rule.

By January 1989, Jaruzelski and Prime Minister Rakowski saw no option but accommodation with Solidarity and the Church—a view that prevailed in the PUWP Politburo only after a Central Committee Plenum filled with rancor and threats of resignation. The Round Table discussion that took place in February and March incorporated many opposition demands, but preserved elements of communist institutional hegemony (e.g., 65 percent of the seats in the Sejm were held, until the next election, by the PUWP and its allied parties). Yet, the obeisance paid to social preferences was clear insofar as the party regime backed away from its long standing intransigence on trade union pluralism, political expression, and other issues.

We should not forget, or course, that all of the tolerance or "liberalization" exhibited by Polish communist regimes was obtained through struggle and confrontation, not the benign neglect of the authorities. Even among Polish intellectuals, there was a long struggle to overcome the isolation imposed by the communist regime.[60] As late as spring 1988, PUWP officials continued to reject notions of institutionalized pluralism (i.e., a multiparty system) because it would lead to "social demagoguery,"[61] while establishment publications attacked suggestions for direct talks between Solidarity leaders and Jaruzelski.[62] Just months before the Round Table accord, the authorities clung to an absolute rejection of both union pluralism and a social contract that would allow some legalization of opposition organizations.

Such an intractable position was, in one tragic sense, quite understandable; unable to submit themselves to a true test in the public sphere, no PUWP regime could move forward toward sanctioned pluralism or backward toward a futile effort to derail social and political opposition.[63] The genie could not be put back into the bottle. Eventually Jaruzelski and

Rakowski took the path of reconciliation with the "established" opposition, hoping that by subsuming Solidarity and the Church within the system their danger to it would be diluted. In 1989, multiple parties, per se, did not compete for all seats in the Sejm or new upper house (Senate). But the effort to buy some time for the PUWP. was truncated by a massive electoral disaster for Polish communists, making clear that Poles despised the PUWP. After two months of uncertainty, Jaruzelski as president had no choice but to turn to a Solidarity figure—Tadeusz Mazowiecki—to form a government.

In Hungary, a change of leadership during the Hungarian Socialist Workers Party (HSWP) conference of May 1988 swept out Janos Kadar, after thirty-two years, more than a third of the Central Committee, and six of eleven Politburo members. Karoly Grosz, whose own role as general secretary was diminished only a year later when a second powerful post of party chairman was created, can fairly be said to have gained his post from "pressure inside and outside the party for greater freedom."[64]

Grosz confronted a rapidly deteriorating economic situation, and a population that, since 1985, had lost much of its positive sentiment toward the system and its performance. To address Hungary's economic doldrums, Grosz had to institute measures that could and did add to the unhappiness of most citizens—cutting government social spending while imposing taxes and raising prices to reduce demand for consumer products.[65]

With such policies, however, had to come compensatory steps aimed toward placating public opinion. As in Poland, the HSWP was loath to relinquish its political monopoly, but was under considerable public and internal pressure in 1988–1989 to give legal status to unofficial groups, and to create a constitutional separation of party and state. Advocates of these steps, specifically Imre Pozsgay and Rezso Nyers, entered the Politburo in 1988 with a substantial mass following. Significantly, it was Nyers to whom HSWP reformists turned as a last hope in June 1989, naming him to a new post—party chairman—that lessened the position of general secretary held by Grosz. Unable to lead in an environment of pluralism and competition, Grosz had failed to keep pace the revolutionary changes moving through Hungarian political life. By the late autumn of 1989, of course, constitutional change, the emotional reburial of Imre Nagy, and changes in East Germany and Poland made Prime Minister Miklos Nemeth little more than a caretaker until the spring 1990 elections.

The HSWP was pushed out by multifaceted and *public* pressures that accumulated after 1985. Particularly in 1988, prior to and after the party conference at which Kadar was removed from office, a number of implicitly

political organizations made their appearance. Each announced an avow-
edly policy-related agenda, and all ignored statutes requiring formal regis-
tration, thereby making an implicit political statement. Western reports at
the time focused on the Federation of Young Democrats (FIDSZ), which
was begun in March 1988 by several dozen students but rapidly extended
its activity into many universities, and the new Democratic Union of
Scientific Workers and Academics, started in May of the same year. A
further 1988 effort to create an umbrella organization uniting "diverse
dissident, environmental, Church and other organizations" was the Network
of Free Initiatives.[67]

By 1989, the "Free Democrat" opposition, led by people such as Janos
Kis and others, had become a powerful force in negotiating with HSWP
leaders. The "Democratic Forum," with perhaps twenty thousand members,
emerged in 1989 as the largest single political organization to rival the
HSWP in elections, although the Smallholders Party was also renewed—
the party that, in 1947, won Hungary's last free parliamentary election
before Soviet coercion stripped away any hope of democracy.

The HSWP's response to the emergence of independent groups and
nascent parties was divided—some leaders showing evident concern while
others applauded such developments. "Socialist pluralism," somewhat like
"democratic centralism," was used by Karoly Grosz to connote limits to
both pluralism and democracy. Grosz used every means at his disposal,
trying to ensure that pluralism did not become rampant, and seeking to
control the proliferation of autonomous associations.

By 1989, however, it was too late to do much more—unless, of course,
the Hungarian regime had been willing and able to engage in massive
repression with Soviet assistance. Grosz, according to individuals in the
Hungarian party establishment, may have *sought* Soviet support for domestic repression, but was rebuffed. At the same time, the emergence of
vehemently antireform HSWP veterans in the "Marxist Unity Platform"
began to imply ominous confrontation. But severe, violent repression was
out of the question. Indeed, even the HSWP's erstwhile chief ideologist,
former Politburo member and Central Committee Secretary Janos Berecz,
spoke about a rethinking of the "link between democracy and socialism"
and of a willingness to enter dialogue with those having different opinions
as long as they "[do] not question the building of socialism."[68]

In early 1989, Berecz and a couple other conservative members of the
Politburo were sacrificed to escalating demands for a new Hungarian
political system, no longer able to constrain the momentum of change. The
regime of Karoly Grosz, however, continued to try to disrupt underground

publishing, by confiscating materials whenever possible and by occasionally detaining leaders of autonomous organizations. Grosz knew all too well, however, that the willing obedience of Hungarians—and their enthusiasm if possible—was required to implement difficult and potentially disruptive reforms that would push the country away from a centrally planned, heavily subsidized system. He also could see, from mass demonstrations in Budapest on March 15, 1988 (the 140th anniversary of the 1848 revolution), however, that popular demands for freedoms and democratic reforms were substantially beyond those a communist party regime could comfortably adopt. Grosz's implicit demotion in June 1989 signaled the HSWP's admission that change could not be contained within intrasystemic reform. Nyers presided, indeed, over the dismantling of party political hegemony.

Although Poland and Hungary, among the six Eastern European allies of the Soviet Union, moved first toward an environment of public legitimation, it would be wrong to assume that even Poles and Hungarians have achieved secure democracies. Clearing out the old *nomenklatura* from social and economic organizations and dismantling the secret police will require decades. But it would be equally wrong to think that the public sphere can now be forced to contract once again.

Elsewhere in Eastern Europe, however, elite-mass relations were not static, and political cultures underwent transformations at different paces with nation-specific variants. The Bulgarian communist government had fewer problems with public support than other Eastern European states through the mid-1980s (see Table 2), and allowed public protests in 1987–1988 concerning air pollution in the border town of Ruse. The object of protests, however, was not Bulgarian authorities, but rather the Ceausescu regime, which had allowed chemical emissions from industrial enterprises and electrical generating facilities across the Danube River boundary to vastly exceed acceptable levels. A February 10, 1988, demonstration in Ruse was reported to have had over two-thousand participants. In early 1989, however, the Zhivkov regime showed its unease about an environmental movement by expelling principal activists and leading human rights protesters. The Bulgarian Communist Party (BCP) had reason to be uneasy, as well, about the volatile issue of the Turkish minority. As Zhivkov confronted further organizational efforts among Turks in spring 1989, and ties between those active for Turkish minority rights in Bulgaria and other issues broadened, the regime countered with an expulsion of more than 300,000 Turks.

The environmental issue, interwoven with opposition to nuclear energy and weapons, began in the late 1980s to foster connections among activists from various Eastern European countries and emboldened their efforts to confront individual governments about objectionable policies.[69] In the latter 1980s, overtly political themes began to diffuse among Eastern European countries as well, and "contacts among dissidents from different countries . . . steadily deepen[ed] and multipl[ied]."[70] Conscientious objection, human rights in the region (e.g., in Romania), religious freedom, workers' rights to have autonomous unions, and so on were all topics for cross-national collaboration.[71]

In Czechoslovakia, activity by Charter 77 broadened into other strata of Czechoslovak society and was given added impetus with large-scale protests in January 1989. Petitions regarding constraints on the Catholic Church, and a growing youth movement that demanded cultural freedom fueled this growing discontent the Czech and Slovak publics. Peace, demilitarization, and nuclear disarmament were also foci for developments that predicted broadened public debate about Czechoslovak commitments within the Warsaw Pact.[72]

When a week of protests took place in mid-January 1989, these same issues recurred, together with chants for "Gorbachev" and "freedom." Czechoslovak police broke up the rallies in Prague's Wenceslas Square with water cannon and truncheons, and trials of prominent dissidents (e.g., Vaclav Havel) took place in subsequent months. Yet, Havel and other Charter 77 personages gained stature, and the Jakes regime was tainted with the indelible memories of brutal police action. These January experiences fed discontent and turned sentiments toward more confrontational strategies. Yet, no dissidents in conversations during January and February imagined the outcomes by late October, and the surrender of power by the party.

The GDR's public opposition was more limited, but the Evangelical Lutheran Church continued to house a large dissident movement with environmental and antiwar sentiments, the actions of which included several demonstrations in early 1988 and substantial protests (petitions and marches) claiming fraud in local elections of spring 1989.[73] The stream of GDR citizens who fled to the West via Hungary in late summer 1989 emboldened the reformists and led to the ouster of Honecker, followed by the succession of Egon Krenz to SED (Communist Party) leadership. Short of Soviet troops acting to halt mounting protests, Krenz could do nothing; the opening of the Berlin Wall, the resignation of Krenz, and massive street protests by the New Forum movement were the death knell of East German communism.

Romanian protest demonstrations escalated in 1987, and took more individual forms in 1988. One event broke out into mass unrest in the city of Brasov on November 15, 1987; perhaps as many as twenty-thousand people participated in protest against Ceausescu and the system, led by workers from the Red Flag truck factory who had gone on strike. This protest, in which the local party headquarters was ransacked, was broken up by secret police and troops. It was, however, only the largest of a series of many demonstrations at universities and large cities throughout 1987 and early 1988,[74] evincing the severe turnaround in Ceausescu's level of public support during the early 1980s, when his regime's performance lost positive evaluations and "gained" negative views more than any other Eastern European state (see Table 1). Antagonism to Ceausescu was never able to coalesce into a substantial dissident movement, but the 1989 protest letters by prominent party members and visible dissenters (e.g., Doinea Cornea in Cluj) raised the level of underground antiregime publishing and other activities.

Precisely how a rebellion against Ceausescu was begun and how it led to his ouster in late December 1989 are debated. Elsewhere, I have detailed contending views and suggested that intraparty dissenters had thought of a conspiracy, but were far from ready to implement it in December. Events in Timisoara and the army's change of heart strongly imply the ad hoc nature of the anti-Ceausescu revolt. The end of his tyranny through popular courage and sacrifice may be the most vivid demonstrations of the depths of their hatred for Ceausescu and clan.

Eastern Europe, then, first saw a revival of "the public's aspirations to participate in politics. People [began] to seek to influence public matters in association with others."[75] Christoph Bertram, writing in *Die Zeit* in May 1988,[76] offered his prescient view that "'democratization' [in Eastern Europe would] soon snowball into a much more fundamental question of power." Bertram noted that the people there are not willing to content themselves with just a few rights of consultation " . . . they want real democracy." Bertram was correct, and the formation of informal groups and their entry into political realms, first effected in Poland, Hungary, and the USSR, intensified rapidly. All ruling communist parties first lost control over policy, and then had to retreat from political leadership. Although Poland and Hungary were first, we then saw this unraveling of communist parties throughout Eastern Europe.

But this exploration and comparison of events suggests a wider "lesson": long before communists lost their ability to insist that subordinates implement their policies, a transition of political culture toward a participatory ethos was effected. Indeed, to accomplish a transition to plural and competitive systems necessitates a new political culture—a new basis of elite-mass relations grounded in public legitimation. But that process began not with the demise of communist rule, but during it. Reform of communist states, as Vladimir Kusin noted, was not about power struggles within the communist bloc's leaderships, but rather about popular participation. The extraordinary irony for those leaderships, however, was that they were both unable to reform without popular participation, *and* unable to retain control with such participation.

IMPLICATIONS FOR POSTCOMMUNIST POLITICS

The transition of political culture described above does not suffice as a basis for pluralistic, competitive democracy. That a country's distribution of attitudes, beliefs, and so on—the substance of political culture—was of greater political consequence in the 1980s than in prior decades provided a basis for 1989 revolutions, but did not insulate new institutions or procedures from reversals.

Changes in the political cultures of states in which communist parties ruled paved the way for revolutions in 1989. The extension of debate about leaders and policies into what T. H. Rigby referred to as the "public political arena," both in the USSR and Eastern Europe, was a development with lasting significance for the political futures of these states. Matters of leadership and policy extruded from the confines of communist parties prior to 1989, and the *nomenklatura* and democratic centralism were unable to again suffice as conceptual boundaries of political life.

Even now, however, the ties of public legitimation to policies are not yet secure. Why popular attitudes and assessments do not translate immediately into clear, direct policy effects is understandable; there is little evidence of such a clear consequence of public opinion in the United States,[77] and one should expect no more in systems newly emerged from rigid authoritarianism.

Public preferences and concerns are generally not fungible assets for politicians in noncompetitive systems. Learning how to "use" public evaluations of leadership or policies effectively, since two generations in Eastern Europe had to concentrate competition on intraparty alignments, will be gradual.

The widening of a public political sphere faster than European communist systems institutionally adapted—with political culture changing faster than formal structures and processes—is consistent with observations made years ago by scholars such as Myron Weiner and Samuel Huntington.

Myron Weiner, of course, wrote of the crisis of the political process represented by political participation that was one in a sequence toward political development.[78] Samuel Huntington's now-classic work *Political Order in Changing Societies* argued, in effect, for institutions to absorb popular demands that are released by socioeconomic changes.[79]

For communist systems in Europe, the institutions of Leninist party rule buckled under the weight of public legitimation. While some of these regimes—Poland and Hungary—were overwhelmed earlier, the others were not immune from similar processes. Even those cases where rulers refused adamantly any compromise with reform, as in Ceausescu's Romania, public antagonism was eventually felt—and all the more vehemently.

No governing experience was provided to, or feasible for, noncommunist intelligentsia prior to the changes of 1989–1990. Political involvement, if present, was generally nonsupportive and confined to the attitudinal dimension. Until the last weeks and days of communist rule in East Germany, Czechoslovakia, Bulgaria, and Romania, political behavior was almost always overtly conformist, while judgments and preferences veered sharply away from regarding socialism as worth anything at all. Condemned to a silent revolution while building a semilegal alternative society, the public political arena grew but not in ways that would create a reservoir of experience in electoral campaigns, legislative work, or local administration—the pragmatic core of democratic systems. In this very important way, a shift in political culture while Leninist parties ruled denied to today's postcommunist governments, perhaps with Poland as an exception, any significant preparatory phase.

New political systems and their still-fragile democratic characteristics are also buffeted by the very expectations of peoples for whom public legitimation came with struggle and sacrifice. These achievements did not come cheaply in human, material, or "psychic" terms, and now there is an adamance on all sides about what is wanted. Poles, Czechslovaks and others will accept no turning back or halfhearted commitment to the people. Knowing simulated change, they want none if it; there is likely to be no patience for committees that study, councils that consult, or an array of local government reorganizations, ministerial reshuffling, or personnel rotations. There is a strong expectation of "real" responsiveness—and there is a willingness to test governments and parties over the long term since, during communist periods, there were many experiences with reforms that were later undone.

Such "real responsiveness" comes at a cost, too, with it clear that initial postcommunist leaders had little more than a truncated "honeymoon," after which expectations were high that institutions *would* act, and that resource allocations *would* change. Where these accomplishments were lacking, patience evaporated rapidly. As a consequence of waiting so long, and absorbing so much abuse from communist governments, the struggle to widen the public political realm now includes an inclination to wait further or compromise anymore.

Every kind of political behavior, therefore, is likely to be invested with firmly held belief. Indeed, it may even be that a kind of purposeful apathy is present in cases such as Poland where exhaustion set in due to the permanence of crisis. In that regard, this is an apathy particularly difficult for a political system to overcome since it was adopted out of a commitment to set aside this arena of life heretofore so futile.

In all of this, there are clear and present dangers. So heightened are expectations that new governments will find it difficult both to pacify those enmeshed in politics *and* to engage those who have purposefully turned their backs on politics. It will be tough to find helping hands.

Further, and most ominous, is the vulnerability of new politicians to irrational appeals. Democracy without mediating institutions, moderating processes, and accommodating attitudes strips away any insulation of governance from demagoguery. In Weberian terms, authority becomes a matter of the charismatic appeal of public figures, obviating the administrative and traditional sources of authority that might provide rational or normative bases for the system. Playing to crowds, not deciding policy, is a tempting route in such an environment.

Public legitimation was the process behind the events of 1989, and that dynamic continues to affect prognoses for new systems emerging in the mid-1990s. While we can applaud the competitive voting, plural outlets for voicing opinions, and enhanced freedom to organize and protest, an enlarged public political sphere is not benign. The revolutions of 1989 were but one stage of a prolonged transformation of elite-mass relations throughout the eastern half of Europe, and we will watch the further unfolding of that process in what is certain to be a turbulent period.

NOTES

1. T. H. Rigby, "A Conceptual Approach to Authority, Power and Policy in the Soviet Union," in *Authority, Power and Policy in the USSR*, T. H. Rigby, Archie Brown, and Peter Reddaway (New York: St. Martin's Press, 1980), 26.

2. Daniel N. Nelson, *Elite-Mass Relations in Communist Systems* (New York: St. Martin's, Press, 1988), 117–138.

3. Karl Marx, "The Class Struggles in France," in Robert C. Tucker, ed., *Marx-Engels Reader*, 2nd ed. (New York: Norton, 1978), 593.

4. Central Intelligence Agency (CIA), *Handbook of Economic Statistics* (Washington, D.C.: CIA, Directorate of Intelligence, 1987), 40.

5. Thad P. Alton, "East European GNP's: Origins of Product, Final Uses, Rates of Growth, and International Comparison," in Joint Economic Committee of the U.S. Congress, *East European Economies: Slow Growth in the 1980s* (Washington, D.C.: U.S. Government Printing Office, 1985), 117.

6. The decline of undecided and "do not know" responses among Czechoslovaks and Poles asked to evaluate the performance of socialism in their country in the late 1970s (1975/76 to 1979/80) was significant—dropping from 23 percent to 12 percent among Czechoslovak respondents and from 20 percent to 13 percent among Poles. See Daniel N. Nelson, "Non-Supportive Participatory Involvement in Eastern Europe," *Social Science Quarterly* 67, no. 3 (September 1986): 636–644.

7. Admonitions by Nicolae Ceausescu were the most blatant. Ceausescu made it abundantly clear, only a half year after Mikhail Gorbachev became CPSU general secretary, that Romania would reject reforms along the lines of those being proposed by the Soviet leader. See, in that regard, Ceausescu's speech to a Romanian Communist Party Central Committee Plenun in November 1985, in *Scinteia* (November 15, 1985). The need for sacrifices so that high levels of investment could be maintained, and the parallel need to increase the state's role in socioeconomic planning, were themes of official media during the mid-to-late 1980s. See, for example, Ceausescu's comments to the Political Executive Committee on April 29, 1988, reported in *Scinteia* (May 4, 1988).

8. At the Hungarian Socialist Workers' Party Conference in late May 1988, for example, the newly elected HSWP leader, Karoly Grosz, made frequent references in his principal speech to the party's relationship with nonsanctioned public organizations and "minority views." Grosz acknowledged that the party must cooperate with views that "serve to benefit socialism but are contrary to the government's position," and promised to follow a principle of nonintervention regarding such organizations. See Judith Pataki, "Grosz and Pozsgay Call for Changes at the Conference," Radio Free Europe, *Hungarian Situation Report* 13, no. 22, SR/7: 33–37.

9. The goal of a civil society, set apart from the world of political conformity dominated by a Leninist party, was inherent to many opposition proposals in Eastern Europe and the USSR. The ability to criticize publicly the political system itself must be a critical test of a "civil society."

10. Different leadership strategies in communist systems were discussed in Daniel N. Nelson, "Charisma, Control and Coercion: The Dilemma of Communist Leadership," *Comparative Politics* (October 1984): 1–16.

11. Gabriel A. Almond and G. Bingham Powell, Jr., "Political Socialization and Political Culture," in Gabriel A. Almond and G. Bingham Powell, Jr., eds.,

Comparative Politics Today: A World View, 4th ed. (Glenview, Ill.: Scott, Foresman, 1988), 40.

12. Gabriel A. Almond and Sidney Verba, *The Civic Culture* (Princeton, N.J.: Princeton University Press, 1963).

13. Lowell Dittmer, "Comparative Communist Political Culture," *Studies in Comparative Communism* 16, nos. 1 & 2 (Spring/Summer 1983): 9–24.

14. Dittmer, 16, 18.

15. Dittmer, 20.

16. Almond and Powell, 41.

17. Ibid.

18. Ibid.

19. Linda L. Lubrano et al., "The Soviet Union," in William A. Wesh, ed., *Survey Research and Public Attitudes in Eastern Europe and the Soviet Union* (New York: Pergamon Press, 1981), 15.

20. Aleksandr K. Orlov, *Trudyashchiyesya v Sisteme Upravleniya Proizvodstvom* (Chelyabinsk: Izdatel'stvo Yuzhno-Ural'skoye, 1976).

21. *Pravda,* February 19, 1988.

22. Mikhail Gorbachev, "Speech to Uzbek Party Leaders," as quoted in Elizabeth Teague, "Gorbachev Counterattacks in Tashkent," RL 161/88, April 13, 1988, in *Radio Liberty Research Bulletin* 32, no. 16 (April 20, 1988).

23. "Gorbachev Votes, Meets Reporter 4 March," *FBIS* (March 5, 1990): 54. *Pravda,* March 5, 1990, 1.

24. Abel G. Aganbegyan, "The Perestroika in Practice," *Review of International Affairs* (Belgrade) 39 (January 5, 1988): 22; Gorbachev's statement, at the June 1988 nineteenth Party Conference, was brought to my attention by Stephen White. See *Pravda,* June 29,1988, 3.

25. Nikolai Shmelev, "Novye trevogi," *Novyi Mir* no. 4 (1988): 160–175.

26. Shmelev, 161–168.

27. George Kennan's comments in *The New York Review of Books* were quoted in *Surviving Together* (Spring 1988): 5–6.

28. Ibid.

29. Jerry Hough, "Gorbachev Consolidating Power," *Problems of Communism* (July–August 1987): 39.

30. *Pravda,* May 14, 1987.

31. Viktor Yasmann, "Glasnost and Soviet Television in 1987," RL 31/88 (January 28, 1988) *Radio Liberty Research Bulletin* 32, no. 5 (February 3, 1988).

32. Ibid.

33. *Current Digest of the Soviet Press* 40, no. 11 (April 13, 1988): 25; see also Sergei Voronitsyn, "When Sociology Connects with Perestroika," RL 166/88 (April 15, 1988) in *Radio Liberty Research Bulletin* 32, no. 16 (20, April 1988).

34. "Leftward Movement Seen in Public Attitudes," *FBIS* (July 5, 1990): 44–45. *Pravda,* January 25, 1990.

35. "Poll Shows Concern over Environmental Issues," *FBIS* (June 21, 1990): 1. *Moscow News* (June 10–17 1990): 7.

36. "Poll on Public Attitudes to Cooperatives," *FBIS* (March 8, 1990): 76. *Izvestiya*, March 3, 1990, 2.

37. Viktor Yasmann, RL 198/88, as summarized in "KGB Goes Public, Publishes Column in Weekly Newspaper to Improve Its Image," *Soviet/East European Report* 5, no. 25 (June, 1, 1988). Yugoslav observers have seen the same tendency in USSR media—the increasing presence of polemics "joined by the broader public," where proponents and opponents of reform seek support from the general public. See "Sources of Current Trends in the Soviet Union," *CSS Papers* (Belgrade: Center for Strategic Studies, 1987): 46–47.

38. S. Frederik Starr, "The Soviet Union: A Civil Society," *Foreign Policy* (Spring 1988).

39. Ibid.

40. *Pravda*, December 27, 1987.

41. Starr.

42. "When the Fishing Had to Stop," *The Economist,* February 6, 1988.

43. Bohdan Nahaylo, "Mounting Opposition in the Ukraine to Nuclear Energy Program," RL Supplement 1/88 (February 16, 1988): 5.

44. Bohdan Nahaylo, "More Ukrainian Scientists Voice Opposition to Expansion of Nuclear Energy Program," *Radio Liberty Research Bulletin* 32, no. 14 (April 6, 1988): RL135/88.

45. "Two Thousand People Protest New Factory," *The Soviet Observer* 1, no. 2 (February 1–15, 1988).

46. Catherine Fitzpatrick and Janet Fleischman, *From Below: Independent Peace and Environmental Movements in Eastern Europe and the USSR* (New York: Helsinki Watch, 1987).

47. David Remnick, "New Soviet Left Emerges," *Washington Post*, March 3, 1988.

48. Aleksandr Minkin, "Zaraza ubiistvennaya," *Ogonok* 13 (1988): 26–27.

49. Ann Sheehy, "Opposition to Family Planning in Uzbekistan and Tajikistan," RL 159/88, April 5, 1988, in *Radio Liberty Research Bulletin* 32, no. 16 (April 20, 1988).

50. "Gorbachev's Tough Stand on Baltic Independence Appears to Have Backfired," *Soviet/East European Report, Radio Free Europe/Radio Liberty* VI, no. 32 (June 1, 1990).

51. Ibid.

52. D. Maslova, "Kak my predstavlyaem sebe demokratiyui glasnost'?" *Argumenty i Fakty* 8 (1988).

53. Almond and Powell discuss the notion of political culture as the distribution of such components, 40.

54. Daniel N. Nelson, "Non-Supportive Participatory Involvement."

55. *The Economist*, May 29, 1988, 63.

56. For example, see International Labor Organization, *World Labor Report, 1987* (Geneva: ILO, 1987): 51.

57. The several *Polacy* studies (national random samples of Poles) undertaken since 1981 have been extraordinary in their scope and attention to methodological precision. See, for example, *Polacy '84*.

58. Jackson Diehl, "The Poles Give a Whole New Perspective to 'Approval' Ratings," *Washington Post Weekly*, January 18–24, 1988.

59. See, for example, the assessment of the ombudsman in "No Shortage of Complaints for Civil Rights Spokesman," RFE Research, *Polish Situation Report* no. 3 (February 25, 1988): 19–23.

60. Jakub Karpinski, "Polish Intellectuals in Opposition," *Problems of Communism* (July-August 1987): 44–57.

61. Interview with Ludwil Drasucki, *Konfrontacje* no. 2 (February 1988).

62. Zygmunt Szeliga, *Polityka*, January 16, 1988.

63. Daniel Passent, "The Spectre of Democracy," *Polityka*, March 26, 1988.

64. This assessment was made in "Round Two in Hungary," *The Economist*, May 28, 1988, 47.

65. Daniel N. Nelson, "Hungary and the Dilemma of Communist States," *Christian Science Monitor*, June 11, 1987.

66. "Independent Political Groups Mushroom," Radio Free Europe Research 13, no. 20, *Hungarian Situation Report* no. 6 (May 20, 1988): 11–15.

67. Ibid., 13.

68. "Ideologist on 'Democracy with Hungarian Sauce'," Radio Free Europe Research 13, no. 12, *Hungarian Situation Report* no. 3 (21 March 1988): 7–8.

69. Brian Morton and Joanne Landy, "East European Activists Test Glasnost," *Bulletin of Atomic Scientists* (May 1988).

70. "A Chain of Change in Gorbachev's Empire," *The Economist*, May 21, 1988, 53–54.

71. Ibid.

72. Peter Martin, "Independent Peace Activity Intensifies," Radio Free Europe Research 13, no. 22, *Czechoslovak Situation Report 8/88* (June 3, 1988): 7–10.

73. Vladimir Kusin, "Dissent in the Streets," *RFE Research Background Report* no. 44, 2–3.

74. Daniel N. Nelson, "The Romanian Party Conference," *Journal of Communist Affairs* 4, no. 3 (July 1988).

75. Vladimir Kusin, "Political Grouping in the Reform Movement," *RFE Research Background Report* no. 89 (26 May, 1988): 2.

76. Christoph Bertram, *Die Zeit*, May 13, 1988.

77. For example, see Robert Weissberg, *Public Opinion and Popular Government* (New York: Prentice-Hall, 1976): 81.

78. Myron Weiner, "Political Participation: Crisis of the Political Process," in Leonard Binder et al., *Crises and Sequences* (Boston: Little, Brown, 1971).

79. Samuel Huntington, *Political Order in Changing Societies* (New Haven, Conn.: Yale University Press, 1968).

Chapter 4

China at the Crossroads: Between Democracy and Dictatorship

LIU BINYAN

The unprecedented 1989 Tiananmen democracy movement in China failed, but the revolution in Eastern European countries succeeded. Two years later, the people of the former Soviet Union discarded their communist regime and many of the successor states have embarked on rudimentary paths toward political pluralism. The communist regime in China, however, seems to be more stable. Why?

A PARTY WITH DEEP ROOTS

The Chinese communists (and perhaps their Vietnamese counterparts as well) are unique among the world's governing communist parties in that they came to power only after more than twenty years of bitter fighting. The honesty and high moral standards they displayed during their first few years in power contrasted so starkly with the darkness and corruption of pre-1949 Kuomintang (KMT) rule that all the unbearable problems that had plagued China for so long seemed to have been obliterated overnight. For the Chinese people, the communists and Mao Zedong became not only great liberators, but the very embodiments of truth, justice, and morality.

Because of the absolute authority and public trust enjoyed by the communists during the 1950s and 1960s, just about every Chinese wanted to join the party. As a result, the best people from every level of society, from the intelligentsia to the commoners, became party members and party cadres. Many of these people may have made numerous mistakes (which they have come to regret), and large numbers of them suffered Mao Zedong's ruthless persecution. When Deng Xiaoping rehabilitated victims of all previous political upheavals in 1979, the former party members who regained their political rights numbered in the hundreds of thousands; many of them again took on leadership duties.

Many middle-aged and older Chinese still remember the communists' outstanding record of political accomplishments during the few short years between 1949 and 1956. This was largely because, even after Mao Zedong led the Chinese people into disasters, many party members and cadres remained committed to their ideals and stood on the side of the people to lessen the effects of those disasters or worked to oppose incompetent or corrupt cadres in the party. This is why the Chinese frequently look at the party from a split perspective. People will occasionally complain, for example, that their local magistrate so-and-so (usually a party member) is "very bad, and ought to be shot, but the local party secretary is a good person; we like him." During the upheavals of 1988 and 1989, people reviled the party from all sides, yet they still would not condone a slogan like "Down with the Communist party!"

THE UNIQUE WAY OF RULING

Mao Zedong learned more from the rulers of Chinese dynasties than from Marx. He packed the traditional Confucian ideology with Marxist jargon, thus satisfying the people's hope for a radical change or revolution. At the same time, he made the people stay loyal and obedient to the communist regime while they wiped out every other kind of commitment. No other communist regime could have controlled the ideology of the whole population to such an extent. While other communist regimes were satisfied if public dissent was absent, the Chinese communist regime went as far as to politicize people's private lives, demanding that individuals sacrifice their personal desires for the party's requirements. Any difference of behavior or thinking from the standards set by the party was regarded as equivalent to sin by the people themselves and was subject to public criticism.

The system itself made all people the slaves of the party's will. Not long after the establishment of the People's Republic of China (PRC), nearly all Chinese adults became employees of the state, except peasants. Independent professionals no longer existed. The freedom to change one's job or to move from one place to another was also gone. Several years later, when the commune system started in the rural areas, nearly 800,000 peasants became slaves of communes.

We must acknowledge that terror was not the principal method of Mao's rule. In the first thirty years of the PRC's history, people were told that the targets of Mao's continuous ideological movements were but a small fraction of the whole population. The majority actually believed what they were told and regarded their real enemies as a minority of recalcitrant capitalists. Through Mao's skillful maneuvers, people were led to believe the party's needs were their own needs. Whenever they sensed that their own interests were violated by the party's policies, they would blame themselves for their own "selfishness," believing that the loyal majority must be always right, not knowing that the majority was thinking the same way. Thus, the brutality starting with campaigns aimed at landlords and capitalists became brutality aimed at the ordinary people by the people themselves. No one dared to voice dissent: fear of the punishment one might receive from the party was reinforced by a more generic fear of being on the wrong side. Condemnation from the society could be much more painful than punishment by the regime.

A dictatorship by the majority against the minority, gradually developing to a dictatorship by the majority against themselves: this ideologically enslaving process is the history of the People's Republic from the early 1950s to the late 1970s. Since workers and peasants were the "masters of the state," naturally they became the main force in attacking the intellectuals—particularly those with independent minds, who dared to speak out for the real interest of the workers and peasants. With the attack escalating through various campaigns, the economic interests and political interests of the attackers—workers and peasants—were infringed upon continuously.

In fact, few workers or peasants actually knew who, exactly, had been the intellectuals. As they blindly followed the Union Communist Party from one ideological campaign to another, they came to the conclusion that this party's authority should never be challenged, and that those who dared to oppose the party never came to a good end. Therefore, in attacking the "rebellious spirit" of the intellectuals, the modicum of rebellious spirit that existed in the hearts of the workers and peasants was suffocated. The traditional mentality of bowing down to authority became the prevailing mentality of hundreds of millions of people. To maintain this, there are representatives of this absolute authority in every village and workshop—the party cadres who have the fate of the peasants and workers in their hands. Consideration for one's personal well-being makes a solid base for the peasants' and workers' fear of the party.

Since 1949, three generations of Chinese intellectuals have been under the cruel persecution of the party. Even today, the persecution has not ceased. In the first thirty years, intellectuals who were punished for their independent minds discovered that, once they were under attack, they would be totally isolated. Such isolation was created in large part because of the deep trust the majority of the people had in the party. Mao was more clever in this respect than Stalin: he usually did not exterminate his political enemies physically. Instead, he labeled them as antiparty, antisocialist, or counterrevolutionary, thereby rationalizing steps that deprived them of all their rights, put them under the surveillance of all the people so that they could serve as "negative examples," and subjected them to constant and persuasive humiliation. These "negative examples" were reminders to the intellectuals that provided an unequivocal warning to be cautious, and never say anything that might displease the party. In 1957, the antirightist papers were helping Mao to warn the intellectuals every day. This was a force strong enough to turn the brave into cowards.

The Cultural Revolution was Mao's political suicide. With the bankruptcy of Mao's ideology, the Chinese people started to wake up to the idea of human rights, and their rebellious spirit began to reemerge. Since the mid-1970s, there have been many protest movements, with the Tiananmen movement of 1989 being the most recent and visible one. It is very hard to imagine that, without any political organization or any independent newspaper responsive to the people, millions of citizens in hundreds of cities would spontaneously take to the streets to protest.

The failure of the 1989 Tiananmen movement was not accidental. The tradition and experience of prior democratic movements since the 1950s, which might have helped activists of the 1980s avoid some dangers, could not be handed down to the younger followers due to the rigid embargo on information. Few of the student leaders on Tiananmen Square had heard of Wei Jingsheng, who has been in jail for ten years just because of his commitment to Chinese democracy. He remained in jail through 1993. In China his name is almost forgotten. But, in New York, he was awarded the Gleisman Human Rights Award in 1993 on the fourteenth anniversary of his imprisonment.

There are more foreigners than Chinese who know the name and deeds of Wei Jingsheng. This may seem unusual. Yet, Wei was convicted by the direct order of Deng Xiaoping. Because Deng's authority cannot be questioned, no one could intercede for Wei, even to mention his name. In the 1980s, two delegations of important Chinese writers visited Paris. When the French stood up to pay respects to Wei Jingsheng, not one of the Chinese writers made any response. They were not necessarily cowards, since they had to protect themselves from being deprived of the right to influence society through their writing. There were, after all, many intellectuals who had already been being forbidden to write and publish. Yet this same reason, we should remember, can also be used as a pretext to cover up one's cowardice.

CHINESE INSTITUTIONS AND POLITICAL FLEXIBILITY

Compared to their Russian counterparts, who were members of the Communist Party of the Soviet Union, Chinese communists are less rigid and dogmatic, and more interested in obtaining practical results. When pursuing a major goal, they are likely to be more flexible on side issues, and at times even willing to make major concessions or accept as a *fait accompli* some elements they dislike. For this reason, people at all levels of the party hierarchy often get away with merely feigning obedience to their superiors.

This means that Chinese political mechanisms are a bit more flexible than those of the Soviet Union. Deng's policy of "holding fast to the four basic principles" (which are hardly distinguishable from Maoism) can thus coexist with his policy of economic liberalization.[1] This is a fundamental aspect of the way Deng Xiaoping (and Chinese people in general) behaves in society: there are some things that one can do but not talk about, while there are other things one merely talks about but does not actually do. Deng has launched "antibourgeois liberalization" campaigns on four separate occasions, yet the freedom enjoyed by the Chinese people is still expanding.[2] Even the centrally planned economic system that has been in force in China for the past several decades has never been as strict as that of the Soviet Union during most of its existence.

Within the areas or departments they supervise, the particular temperaments and attitudes of individual Chinese leaders can often depart from the restrictions established by the system and its policies. A few months after Mao Zedong launched an intensive nationwide campaign of agricultural collectivization in 1956, for example, a county party-committee secretary in Zhejiang province dared to propose a plan for setting farm output quotas on the basis, not of communes, but of individual households (*baochan dao hu*), and the Zhejiang provincial party-committee secretary dared to implement it temporarily, even if only on a trial basis. (This system was one that Deng himself dared not fully authorize even as late as 1979.)

Situations like this became even more common after the Cultural Revolution. The chaos of that period had brought the activities of the party organization to a halt for as long as five years, and all party cadres were subjected to ruthless ideological denunciations. As a result, the will and morale of the Chinese Communist Party, previously known for its "iron discipline," were enormously damaged. Different political factions arose within the party, and corruption among party cadres worsened significantly. All of this had a devastating impact on the original political and economic system, but it also led to significant liberalization inside the party even before Deng launched his reforms. This partially explains why there was less resistance from within the party to those reforms than there was from within the Soviet Communist Party to reforms in that system.

These distinctive aspects of Chinese political practice are among the reasons why the Chinese communists have been able to find ways out of their crises and avoid total collapse.

BEHIND THE RAPID GROWTH

China has indeed succeeded in generating rapid economic growth, contrasted sharply with the economic difficulties and political instability of Russia and the Eastern European countries. But most China observers ignore a critical question: to whom should we pay tribute for all these achievements?

Let's look back at the time immediately after the June massacre in 1989. A dramatic setback took place in all fields of personal and political freedom. A severe attack on anything "bourgeois" occurred and all dissent was efficiently silenced. Thousands of factories were closed due to economic stagnation brought about by the decision of the hard-liners to eliminate all things representing "bourgeois tendencies," including private enterprises. The result was massive unemployment and widespread strikes.

It was precisely the fear of the reemergence of a protest movement like the Tiananmen movement and the resistance of reform-minded forces within the party that made the party leaders hesitate in pursuing the over-all return of the party conservatives. Deng then discovered to his consternation that the ultimate target of the attack on "bourgeois tendencies" was actually himself. At the same time, the Eastern European countries collapsed one by one. To avoid the same fate, Deng started cautiously to return to the reform lines that had been evident before the June 4 massacre. Finally, in the spring of 1992, Deng decided that the time was ripe for a counterattack on the hard-liners.[3] His counterattack, however, was strictly limited to the economic sphere, carefully avoiding any step beyond into political issues.The so-called economic boom, together with the superficial stability of the society, has misled not only foreign observers but even the Chinese themselves. Some Chinese have said: "Development in China is now quite satisfactory. Just let it run its course. We must not push the government to undertake political reform. It will occur naturally, when the time comes." But, it will be miraculous if this prediction comes true. Much to our regret, the reality in China indicates just the opposite.

It is amazing to see that prophets have forgotten not only that the crises leading to the outbreak of Tiananmen demonstrations have gone unresolved. Many alarm signals coming from China even in the economic sphere have been ignored.

First, Chinese economic life in recent years is full of anomalies. It is really hard to imagine a country with such a huge population having most of its citizens engaged in business. Almost all adults in the cities, including artists, writers, professors, government and party officials, military officers, students, workers, and peasants are involved in some business. Money seems to be made easily. Within months, the value of some stocks has soared to five hundred times their original value. Some people can become millionaires overnight. Workers in state-run factories receive salaries, and bonuses in cash or other forms of payments, even though their factory might have operated at a loss or stopped production for months or even years. With the revenue of the state steadily diminishing, private wallets are swelling faster and faster.

With the building of new factories and the movement of factories to the mainland from Hong Kong, with foreign investments and manufacturing techniques pouring in, and with the intelligence and diligence of the Chinese people liberated by economic reform, China is unquestionably getting wealthier and wealthier.

But, along with this trend, another process is under way. That process is the looting of the accumulated wealth created by the workers and peasants in the past decades—a wealth owned by the state. These resources were accumulated during years of extreme hardship when people had to work under harsh circumstances, often without sufficient food and clothes to keep them fed and warm. Investigations made in the late 1970s found that, in many peasant families, the total property of the family after decades of hard work amounted to the equivalent of only three U.S. dollars. The condition of the urban dwellers was better, but people still lived under very difficult conditions. It was not uncommon that a professor or a writer was unable to find a place to put his desk in his home because it was too small.

Of course not all people who are engaged in business can get rich. Those who had the good fortune to be among the first batch of passengers on the "train to get rich earlier" were children of high-ranking officials. Starting from the end of the 1970s, foreign trade, arms sales, military supplies, and the domestic trade of rare metals and raw materials gradually came to be dominated by these "princes" and princesses."[4] With the establishment of stock markets, and the beginning of sales of state-owned land and real estate, a wonderland of boundless resources for speculation emerged before their greedy eyes. Deng Xiaoping's eldest son, Deng Pufang, is the preeminent figure on the stock exchange, and his brother Deng Zhifang is in the real estate business. Who else in China can compete with them?

The existence of a bureaucratic capitalist class in China is already a reality. In the 1940s, Mao Zedong referred to the bureaucratic capitalist class in the KMT as one of the "three massive mountains sitting on the heads of the Chinese people."[5] What name, then, should we give to this newly emerged bureaucratic capitalist class within the Communist Party? What distinguishes the new class from the one in the 1940s is that the new class is far larger in scale and is also much more overpowering.[6] It is beyond any law, and outside of any scrutiny by the public and mass media. Had their KMT counterparts been present today, they would envy this new class for their "freedom" in gaining personal profits.

In contrast to those who were born with silver spoons in their mouths, ordinary citizens who depend solely on their salaries can hardly make ends meet.[7] These are the teachers, professors, government workers, and party clerks, and the majority of the forty million workers in the state-owned sector. Their jobs offer them no opportunity for bribes, and their expertise, if there is any, offers them no possibility for a second profession. They have no spare money to invest, no way to make extra money, and they are always worried about how to get by.

Peasants make up to 70 to 80 percent of the entire Chinese population.[8] Since the early 1950s, the peasants have been made to bear the brunt of costly disasters brought about by the willful mistakes of Mao and other policy makers. Since the peasants have been docile and silent, the authorities do not pay much attention to their grievances. But, urban dwellers must be dealt with more cautiously, because any open protest can destroy the fragile stability the regime tries so hard to maintain. Therefore, subsidies were handed out to city people to pacify their anger over inflation, while wages were kept the same no matter how much loss the state-owned factories incurred.

All these expenses to subsidize living standards in cities were paid by taxes from the peasantry. Indeed, even without the burden imposed by the government, the peasants must hand over a large share of their income to keep the local and grassroots party cadres well paid. In a village in Shandong province, for example, the secretary of the village party cell receives 3,500 Yuan (RMB) a year, which is higher than a professor's salary. In Heilongjiang province, in northeast China, the head of a village party cell receives almost the same salary as his counterpart in Shandong. Beside this 3,500 yuan, he also gets substantial bribes from those seeking his assistance in their personal need.

A figure published at the beginning of the 1990s showed that the proportion of peasants' income being taken by the state in one way or another increased at the rate of 22 percent each year; simultaneously, the gross income of peasants virtually stagnated. Moreover, at the end of the 1980s, peasants were unable to get cash payments for the grain they sold to the government. Instead, they received IOUs from the government, most of which could not be cashed for some time.

Year after year, Chinese peasants have endured the injustice of an undemocratic system. As a consequence, more and more peasants began to take justice into their own hands. Beginning in 1987, a number of attacks against the local party cadres were reported or rumored to have occurred.[9] Although in June 1989 this trend slowed temporarily, more widespread and drastic uprisings by peasants seem now to be possible as the momentum for rural unrest is rekindled.

CHINA WILL MAKE ITS OWN CHOICE

A peaceful and gradual transition to democracy is still possible in China. A clear majority of Chinese hope for such a future. But the death of Deng Xiaoping (generally expected to occur within the next year or two) may remove a major factor in China's stability, while simultaneously stirring up other destabilizing forces.

A full-scale civil war does not appear likely; due to regional differences in development and local sociopolitical conditions, change in China will take place at varying paces and will adopt diverse forms in each province and region. Prospects for peaceful change in China will be greatest in the coastal areas, while varying degrees of disturbances and disorder appear to be inevitable in inland areas. In fact, two rebellious outbreaks at the county seat level occurred at the outset of 1993.

It is an illusion to think that China can become another Singapore or Taiwan by relying solely on economic growth with political reform and democratization. Those who cling to this illusion ignore two major characteristics of China.

First, mainland Chinese are different from Chinese living anywhere else in the world; more than forty years of Chinese communist rule have cut them off from the cultural tradition that has been preserved by the worldwide Chinese diaspora. Mao Zedong successfully wiped out the sources of authority that have traditionally maintained stability in China throughout its history, replacing them with the party as sole authority; now, however, such a unique source of authority has vanished as well. Today, the only internal source of authority in the minds of the mainland Chinese is their own personal instincts and desires.

At the same time, the Chinese communists also attacked social morality and religion, destroyed education, and left the law so compromised that it no longer commands respect. Thus, there are neither internal nor external restrictions on a Chinese person's behavior. The corruption of party and government officials drives the corruption of the entire society.

For more than forty years, Mao Zedong pushed the Chinese people toward a political awakening by imposing his rigid ideological precepts. Twice he pushed them into a hopeless impasse: during the 1956–1961 famine, and during the Cultural Revolution.[10] He stripped them of all their freedoms, stifled their hopes, and gave them no choice but to become the party's "docile tools." Precisely because he did his job too well, the Chinese people have only now awakened from their sleep of several thousand years and realized that they are human beings with a right to defend their personal freedoms, to pursue their individual interests, and to seek their individual development. Deng Xiaoping's reforms further loosened the bonds imposed on individuals by the communist system and its ideology.

Chinese society has such abundant energy now because of this realization combined with Deng's economic reforms. This energy can be a constructive force or a frighteningly destructive one, however. The Chinese people are no longer abjectly obedient to anyone who tramples them, which is an enormous and historic step forward. But, some Chinese officials say that the Chinese have become "cunning and violent"—an evaluation that is quite true insofar as the people are much smarter now and also much braver.

Today's Chinese population would never accept the kind of autocratic leadership and doctrine practiced by Prime Minister Lee Kuan Yew of Singapore, nor would they submit to Singapore's coercive social system.

Western observers may not agree with these arguments. Praise for Deng based on the economic miracles he "created" is frequent. At the same time, non-Asian analysts often worry about what will happen in the aftermath of Deng's death. Western journalists, scholars, and government analysts all ponder how long China will remain stable in a post-Deng era.[11]

One of the most important reasons why the communist regime in China has been able to maintain its rule after the Tiananmen massacre is the absence, until now, of any credible alternative political force strong enough to challenge the regime. At the same time, the rigid news embargo imposed by the communist authorities makes it very difficult for the Chinese people to learn the truth about the world and China itself, or to know about China's crises and where opportunities for peaceful change may lie.

In the Maoist era, people were forbidden to have any organizations of their own; even nonpolitical societies were banned. This policy has not changed in the Deng era. Some twenty years later, a human rights movement is still forbidden. The desire for political participation has been suffocated again and again. The Communist Party is beyond remedy, yet there is no alternative force in which people might place their trust. These are the reasons why the Chinese people are so frustrated and depressed about China's political future, notwithstanding the appearance of economic prosperity in coastal cities. The intellectuals of China still cannot form an independent social force, which poses yet one more obstacle on the way to democracy.

CONCLUSION

The fundamental barrier faced by China's democractic movement is the lack of a theory. Chinese democrats see before them no clear road to democracy that would be suitable to China's unique conditions; intellectuals have not engaged in thinking about how popular mobilization for democratic goals can be achieved and have not assessed how to make them see hope and have trust in China's future. The hardships and chaos after the revolutions in the former Soviet Union and Eastern Europe, and the economic recession and corruption in politics in the West, have made a deep impression on the Chinese people. The Chinese are worried about the possible consequences of political reform, and some are even ready to accept compromises with the communist regime because of their fear of turmoil in China. This silent but efficient corrupting of Chinese society is pursued aggressively by the party, which plays on such fears and offers compensatory benefits for those who choose to compromise their values.

A great experiment of historical significance is unquestionably taking place in China. It is possible that someday, the miracle of Chinese democracy may take place. But this miracle will certainly not be the one that some observers predict, that is, that democracy will develop on its own accord if the present regime is left alone to pursue economic reform and marketization.

If China is fortunate enough to draw necessary lessons from the former Soviet Union and Eastern European countries, if Chinese intellectuals will devote their energy to identify a path appropriate to democracy for China, and if the international community will devote vigorous attention to China's human rights record, then China may avoid some obstacles on their way to democracy. But, between the fall of the totalitarian regime and the establishment of a democratic, prosperous, and stable society, there will certainly be a prolonged period of hardships. We will have to pay a high cost, particulary since no one can be confident that a peaceful, gradual evolution will not be interrupted by turmoil following Deng's death.

NOTES

1. The "four basic principles" to be upheld are the socialist road, the dictatorship of the proletariat, the Communist Party leadership, and the leading role of "Marxism-Leninism–Mao Zedong thought."

2. Chinese leaders spare little effort in making it clear that the nation needs to safeguard itself against "bourgeois liberalization," a phrase referring to the democracy movements and liberal thoughts among Chinese intellectuals. To the hard-liners in Beijing, "bourgeois liberalization" is a Western plot aimed at weakening the current Chinese regime through peaceful evolution, and thus represents a security threat to China's sovereignty. For a thorough elaboration of "bourgeois liberalization" from Beijing's perspective, see Wang Renzhi's "Opposition to Bourgeois Liberalization," *Beijing Review*, April 23, 1990, pp. 17–27, and An Zhiguo's "Why Does China Oppose Bourgeois Liberalization?" *Beijing Review*, February 12, 1990, pp. 18–21.

3. On April 3, 1992, there was a call by the National People's Congress in China to guard against "leftism," marking a counterattack by the reformers, led by Deng Xiaoping, against the hard-liners, led by Prime Minister Li Peng. (See Nicholas D. Kristof's "China Take Jab at 'Leftists' and Nudges Economy," *The New York Times*, April 4, 1992, p. A2). On May 2, Chen Yun, China's most influential conservative, made his first public appearance in a year to offer an endorsement of the current campaign for more rapid economic reform. (See Sheryl WuDunn's "Chinese Hard-Liner Gives the Nod to Freer Market," *The New York Times*, May 3, 1992, p. 11).

4. "Princes" and "princesses" mainly refer to the children of China's high-ranking officials. Depending upon powerful connections and their partents' authority, they become millionaires or billionaires through trading in stocks, rare materials, or real estate.

5. The other two "massive mountains" are imperialism and feudalism.

6. The "New Class" here refers to the new class of Chinese entrepreneurs and consumers who have recently become affluent as a result of Deng's "open" and "reform" policy. Most of these nouveaux-riches are children of the Chinese leaders—that is, the "princes and princesses," who use their family backgrounds and connections to net personal gains.

7. The Chinese usually live on their salaries. However, in recent years more and more incomes come from a second profession. For those with relations, good contacts, and access to bribery, real incomes are much higher than the nominal salaries. Consequently, income gaps between the urban rich and poor, rural and urban areas, and coastal and inland areas have widened alarmingly. In 1990, Shanghai's per capita annual income was RMB 5,570 yuan (approximately $1,000), while that of Guizhou was only 780 yuan ($140); see *China Statistical Yearbook* (1992). Taking the 1990 rural per capita income of less than RMB 300 yuan ($54) as an indicator of abject poverty, no fewer than 8.7 percent of peasant households, more than 65 million people, fall in this category (*The Economist*, November 28, 1992).

8. According to the Statistical Communiqué of the State Statistical Bureau of China (SSB), by the end of 1993 China's total population numbered 1,185.17 million, with a natural growth rate of 11.45 per thousand. This figure represents an increase of 13.46 million over the 1992 figure.

9. The influential riot was in Renshou county of Sichuan province, in which approximately ten thousand people participated. This riot was primarily fueled by higher local levies and corruption. Trying to ameliorate rising rural discontent, the central government in late June of 1993 announced the cancellation of thirty-seven taxes and fees, including "social stability fees" and land registry taxes.

10. The so-called Great Proletarian Cultural Revolution was a great disaster for the Chinese. It brought about a RMB 500 billion yuan loss; see *China Statistical Yearbook* (1984). It resulted in China's social and political decay, as well as the Communist Party's loss of general hegemony over ideology and legitimacy.

11. Some Western analyses predict a troubled political succession after Deng's death. "There is no clear successor, and jockeying for the top job when Deng dies could cause instability" (*The Wall Street Journal*, December 10, 1993, R19). "The power of Mao's designated successor, Hua Guofeng, lasted only two years after the Great Helmsman passed away in 1976. Mr. Deng's death will probably set off a power struggle as big and vicious as the one that took place then" (*The Economist*, November 28, 1992).

Chapter 5

The Fragility of Democracy:
The Case of Zaïre

FLORIBERT CHEBEYA

Twenty years after achieving independence, most African countries have a monolithic political system dominated by a single party. Africa's tendency toward one-party control began, in most cases, with one of the factions engaged in the struggle for independence asserting its dominance over rival factions. In an alleged effort to counter internal conflict during postindependence consolidation, one-party rule became a common theme throughout the continent.

In the case of Zaïre, also called Congo-Kinshasa, President Joseph-Desire Mobutu took power on November 24, 1965, through a military coup against President Joseph Kasa-Vubu, who had been proclaimed president by the Belgian colonizers on June 30, 1960. President Mobutu slowly built and consolidated a dictatorship led by a single party, the Popular Movement of the Revolution (MPR).

Mobutu's dictatorship has been characterized by the systematic violation of human rights as defined in the articles of the United Nations' Universal Declaration of Human Rights.[1] His regime is an inhumane, repressive machine marked by the institutionalization of corruption at all levels. The people have been excluded from the management of the country and have become increasingly impoverished. President Mobutu became the absolute leader of the country. He has ruled in a fashion unchecked by legal or moral norms, embezzling public funds resulting from national production and accepting monetary and material gifts as well as credit from foreign countries. During the Cold War, President Mobutu also benefited from Western military assistance.

Driven by the tragedy of the situation, many citizens of Zaïre have dared to protest both individually and collectively. The government has responded with imprisonment, physical and psychological torture, assassinations, poisonings, professional dismissals, banishment of students, arbitrary closings of universities, deportations within the country, kidnappings, disappearances, and so on.

This tragic situation was fertile ground for a group of students and intellectuals who, revolted by the dictatorship in power, risked their lives to create the "Voice of the Voiceless." This group attempted to increase popular awareness of fundamental human rights through an underground bulletin called *The Voice of the Voiceless: Journal of the Oppressed of Zaïre.* The group organized visits of compassion and information to prisons, and offered material and legal assistance to political prisoners, all in the utmost secrecy.[2]

DEMOCRACY: BIRTH AND DEVELOPMENT, APRIL 1990 TO THE PRESENT

Mobutu Rejects Democratic Change

Under the influence of strong internal and external pressures, and also of Soviet *perestroika* and its subsequent effect on other dictatorships, President Mobutu was forced to announce the institution of "democracy" in a televised speech delivered at Kinshasa-N'sele on April 24, 1990. Earlier Mr. Mobutu, unruffled by the winds of *perestroika*, had traversed the provinces of Zaïre on a campaign of "popular consultation," during which he collected opinions regarding the past, present, and future role of state institutions.

As a result of these consultations, Mobutu promised support for increased democracy in his address to the nation on April 24, 1990, after which the people demanded the implementation of simple institutional reforms. President Mobutu's promise of democracy was received joyously by the populace, which organized spontaneous public marches throughout Zaïre.

Contradictions were revealed immediately, however, in an interview accorded the foreign press on April 24, 1990, and in a presidential speech delivered to the National Assembly on May 3, 1990. In these pronouncements, President Mobutu virtually retracted all essential elements of his promise to the nation for democratization. This "clarification" speech abruptly halted the popular rejoicing. The populace launched protest movements to signal its disapproval. Students staged demonstrations at Kinshasa, Lubumbashi, and other cities in Zaïre. During the night of May 12, 1990, the government struck back. After regional authorities first cut all electricity, students from the University of Lubumbashi in Shaba (Katanga) were brutally massacred.

In order to weaken President Mobutu, the population, which still desired democracy, resolved to resist peacefully. During the next several months, people struggled ceaselessly for the presidential creation of a national conference. This conference was seen as the most effective means to peaceful democratization of the country. Weary of war, President Mobutu yielded, but refused to disarm. Thus, he stubbornly resisted the authority of the National Sovereign Conference (CNS) before, during, and after its attempts at reform.

His resistance was vehement, particularly regarding the Conference's act that stipulated constitutional provisions for a two-year transition to democracy. This act provided for the cooperation of three principal institutions during the transition: The presidency, a High Council of the Republic (HCR), and the government. Mr. Mobutu, however, chose to use the army to paralyze and revoke the government instituted by the National Sovereign Conference. He arbitrarily closed the Conference, prevented the High Council from meeting, and took members of the National Assembly hostage for three days.[3]

In March 1993, President Mobutu met in Kinshasa with a political group called the Réconciliation Nationale, which was in favor of "rectifying" the act regarding constitutional provisions for the transition period, as well as setting dates for a constitutional referendum and presidential and legislative elections.

By mid-1993, two governments existed in Zaïre—one led by Etienne Tshisekedi (designated by the National Sovereign Conference and the High Council of the Republic) and the other led by Faustin Birindued (designated by the political symposium of Kinshasa). Such political chaos, coupled with a background of corrupt authoritarianism, bodes ill for Zaïre's future.

The People's Judgment

In the eyes of the population, the constitution governing the country under the current institutional dictatorship is invalid. The document is perceived as the manifestation of President Mobutu's wishes and as giving him full control. Mobutu, meanwhile, regards this constitution alone as valid, and continues to consult it. As for the global political compromise negotiated by the political parties during the meanderings of the National Sovereign Conference, the constitutional act pertaining to the transition period continues to be contested by the president. Mobutu insists on the necessity of harmonizing the entire text in order to avoid a conflict-ridden transition period.

Political parties have, in such an environment, proliferated. But most of these parties lack a popular base. Many opportunists found themselves at the head of such false parties, which became political cartels nourished by President Mobutu. Some parties and political cartels did engage in constructive efforts to mobilize the population and to engage them in political life. These efforts, however, quickly died due to organizational, material, and financial difficulties.

Since April 24, 1990, Zaïre has been torn apart by two diametrically opposing ideologies: the popular desire for democratization, and Mobutu's desire to maintain the status quo.

In 1991, the opposition was unable to succeed in organizing civil disobedience movements and strikes; the population was momentarily distracted by monetary investments financed by the president's party. Cash payments and other inducements obscured, for a time, the nation's true needs. However, on February 16, 1992, and March 1, 1992, two peaceful demonstrations were organized by religious organizations in Kinshasa. The army intervened, violently repressing the demonstrations and firing upon the mob. Many people were killed, wounded, tortured, or arrested; many disappeared. The army again opened fire on peaceful demonstrators in Kinshasa on December 14 and 18, 1992, who were protesting the regime's failure to democratize. In an attempt to show its disapproval and its rejection of President Mobutu, the population of Kinshasa protested in the main streets of the city, particularly the Boulevard du 30 Juin.[4]

Control and Resistance in Mobutu's Zaïre

Mass media have become the quickest and surest means of alienation and moral deprivation. In Zaïre, the official radio and television stations have a monopoly; there are no private radio or television stations in the country. The mass media remain the exclusive tool of the government, which uses print and broadcast outlets in an abusive and slanderous manner. Democracy has not yet touched the official radio and television stations. Only the proceedings of the National Sovereign Conference receive coverage from the official stations. Most internationally accredited journalists have been barred, suspended, or dismissed from the Zaïre Office of Radio and Television (OZRT). These journalists, earmarked "dangerous" by the OZRT, created a group called "Association for a Responsible and Democratic Audiovisual Media" (APARO).

In contrast, several private newspapers were founded in order to seek Zaïre's rapid democratization. Caricatures and criticisms of President Mobutu dominated these private newspapers. These newspapers are often the target of surveillance, vandalism, and forced entry by government forces, and journalists are frequently intimidated. The private press is confronted with difficulties such as the lack of primary materials, as well as the low purchasing power of the population. Because of the struggle against the private press, salespeople who sell these underground publications often risk their lives. The military is frequently dispatched to disperse these salespeople and engages in numerous activities to prevent the distribution of these newspapers.

Despite the promises of democratization made by President Mobutu, foreign journalists continue to face difficulties, particularly with the military, in their radio and television reports on the situation in Zaïre. In March 1993, journalists of the Africa News Service and International Television London had a bitter experience. Zaïre's diplomatic missions abroad refused to authorize visas for journalists and human rights activists declared *persona non grata* by Mobutu's regime. At Kinshasa's Mdjili Airport, the National Office of Immigration (ANI), armed to the teeth, resorted with increasing frequency to arbitrary detentions of foreign travelers before expelling them in an inhumane manner.

Since April 14, 1990, popular resistance against Mobutu's dictatorship has paralyzed the country. Workers and government employees suffer from a lack of motivation, and any economic activity capable of generating revenue barely exists. Production has largely ceased. Each month, the government resorts to vouchers to pay its workers' salaries. Hyperinflation is rampant, purchasing power declines daily, and misery increases.

In December 1992, the president of the republic and the governor of the central bank decided to issue a new currency, zaïres, and to force five million zaïres into circulation. The population rejected this worthless currency, which was printed at the expense of human lives. Once again, the presidential party utilized the Special Presidential Division of the military (DSP) and the National Guard to impose the currency on the population. Dozens of people were beaten, wounded, arrested, and tortured as they fought to protect their families' economic survival.

Since the beginning of Zaïre's democratization process, the country's poverty has become more and more pervasive. It is well-known that under Mobutu's dictatorship Zaïreans live on their resourcefulness, not their salaries, the size and dependability of which are entirely inadequate for survival. However, this resourcefulness has ceased to sustain the people, who live by the miracle of God. The country is dying. Nothing functions: roads are impassable, banks are without cash, the postal and banking services are chaotic, medical services are almost nonexistent, civil servants have not been paid since October 1992, and the universities have been closed for two years. The remnants of society thus lie battered and strewn about, with few prospects of even the most modest improvement.[5]

Since April 24, 1990, the armed forces have frequently reached for the trigger. Certain units of the army are occasionally disarmed to benefit the Special Presidential Division and the National Guard. These units are the Pretorian Guard under the direct command of persons close to Mobutu. It is a widely held belief that the latter units are in the exclusive service of President Mobutu against the people of Zaïre. The army mutinied in September and October of 1991, and engaged in looting which destroyed the remainder of the country's economy. What was one of Africa's most promising cases of economic development has now sunk into ruin.

Today, the man in uniform unsettles more than he protects. Legitimate and illegitimate armed forces have created a permanent atmosphere of terror and insecurity which traumatizes the population. These armed forces have transformed Zaïre into a jungle of armies.

Organizations for the defense of human rights and their members operate in an atmosphere of danger and insecurity. The president remains insensitive to the pressure exerted on the government by these organizations. Despite the risks involved, the organizations continue to promote programs designed to raise public awareness of human rights, supported in many cases by grants from Europe, Japan, and North America. These programs provide moral, social, material, and medical assistance to victims of human rights abuses.

The international community is often misinformed, and even more often uninformed, about the serious sociopolitical situation in Zaïre. This is the result of a very weak and costly communication system which inhibits communication within Zaïre as well as with the outside world. Merely making an international telephone call is functionally impossible without alternative satellite links. Such inaccessibility of communication, of course, both insulates Zaïrian repression from global scrutiny and places a heavier burden on local, indigenous opposition to Mobutu.

Due to the blockage of democratic processes within Zaïre, certain Western diplomatic missions, such as that of Canada, are in the process of completing their current business in the country and closing their doors. Other diplomatic missions are following Canada's lead.

Western governments must recognize their partial responsibility for the serious situation in Zaïre. For approximately twenty years, these governments, for various reasons—often misguided because of Cold War confrontations—supported Mobutu. He was accorded substantial military and financial assistance by the United States and Western Europe. This aid contributed to the creation of a financial oligarchy controlled by Mobutu, as well as to a strong military arsenal which the president currently uses against the people of Zaïre.

FUTURE ACTION

On the national level, President Mobutu continues to refuse to participate in the democratization process defined by the National Sovereign Conference, thereby remaining the major obstacle to democratization. Considering that further rational political negotiation is impossible and that President Mobutu, due to his repeated attempts to block democracy, represents a great public danger, the people of Zaïre must concentrate their effort on ejecting Mobutu from office. Such an effort must be mounted from within Zaïre with the support of the international community.

In order to guarantee the process of democratization in Zaïre, the decisions and recommendations made by the National Sovereign Conference must be implemented. Given the high number of human rights violations committed by Mobutu's army and the extreme misery of the population, it has become acutely important to support morally, politically, and materially the HCR and the government created by the National Sovereign Conference.

On the international level, it has been established that President Mobutu clings to power on the strength of stolen wealth and military force. His theft of perhaps billions of dollars from national income and foreign assistance is well documented. Western nations have understood this, and have taken restrictive and coercive measures against Mobutu. In recent years, they have suspended cooperation and military assistance, refused visas to members of the government, and frozen or seized Mobutu's foreign assets.[6]

In order to guarantee the process of democratization in Zaïre, an international military presence is needed in order to prevent further genocide. Such a humanitarian assistance project must focus on helping the victimized population of Zaïre. We advocate strong multilateral action that would impose a renewed security within Zaïre based upon respect for human rights.[7]

CONCLUSION

Zaïre's road to democratization broke down mainly due to the position of President Mobutu, and his efforts to concentrate all real power in the country in his hands. The president's desire to achieve this goal reduced human life and dignity to precariously low levels.

The case of Zaïre, exposed in this manner, is an example to avoid. It is essential that the population of Zaïre, like people throughout the world, remain firmly convinced of the good of democracy. This deep conviction enables the people of Zaïre to continue struggling, both inside the country and abroad, for a just and democratic future.

Despite the difficulties and the high cost, I and my organization believe that chances for democratization and socioeconomic improvement in Zaïre are great. The country possesses potential, diverse resources, and a population which clings firmly to its optimism. In these positive factors, we place our hope and energy. We shall continue our struggle.

NOTES

1. United Nations Information Department, *Déclaration universelle des droits de l'homme,* Article 1.

2. Malange Kalunzu Maka, *Prêtres dans la rue* (Kinshasa: Editions Baobab, 1992), 100.

3. La Voix de sans Voix pour les Droits de l'Homme, *Check-up sur l'état de la démocratisation au Zaïre, du 24 avril 1990 au 31 décembre 1991* (Kinshasa: VSV, 1991).

4. Comité Droits de l'Homme, Maintenant, *Appel aux autorités de notre pays,* February 1993, p. 3.

5. "Folly by Numbers," *The Economist,* August 7, 1993.

6. "Three Western Nations Demand Zaire Leader Yield Power," *The New York Times,* February 4, 1993.

7. Comité Droits de l'Homme, Maintenant, *Pour une force internationale d'interposition du Zaïre,* February 17, 1993, p. 2.

Part II

Security and Democracy:
European and Global
Perspectives

After authoritarianism, transitions that could lead toward democracy or disorder are affected by many factors, principal among which is the degree of security available to the new systems. Historically, the genesis of plural, tolerant, and competitive polities has been a long, conflictual process. During that extended period—decades if not centuries—geographic insulation, inexhaustible resources, or protection by a larger patron have played a role in ensuring ample capacities with which to meet threats.

Absent a dynamic balance between threats and capacities, democrats are unlikely to arise, or stay democrats for very long. Unless a political system's capacities can balance real or perceived threats, attachment to democratic norms is less than certain in the face of more urgent needs. Demogogues can appeal to base instincts by arguing that tenets of democracy such as personal freedoms, rule of law, and social tolerance are unaffordable luxuries.

Today, threats are multiplying, not subsiding. No longer do we or our allies concern ourselves about communist subversion, Warsaw Pact or Soviet-inspired aggression, or similar overt dangers. Instead, fears of international organized crime, terrorism, ethnic unrest and conflict, nuclear proliferation, mass migration, and other transnational threats have become omnipresent, for Europeans, Asians, and people elsewhere.

Particularly in Europe, but on other continents as well, the late 1980s and early 1990s offered an opportunity to inaugurate transitions to stable democracies. Yet, voices were quickly raised from new leaders in Central, Eastern, and post-Soviet Europe that an end to communism meant the rise of an enlarged array of threats endangering fledgling governments.

How can established Western democracies help to provide an environment of security in which nascent postauthoritarian systems' progress can be nurtured? Are there institutions and policies that can accelerate or ease building tolerant, plural, and competitive norms where those ideas have long been suppressed?

In Part II, contributions by Simon Serfaty, Regina Karp, Charles William Maynes, and Admiral Paul David Miller all address security dilemmas of the late 1990s to the early part of the next century. Each of these analysts devotes particular attention to reinforcing stable postauthoritarian transitions with new or existing multilateral structures, and with U.S. foreign and national security policy.

They chart no simple course. Indeed, all four chapters point unswervingly toward the heightened complexities surrounding all assessments and policy making now that unambiguous adversaries and clear-cut hegemony are gone. For Serfaty, that which is "Europe" has become coextensive with the security that being in Europe connotes—and there is ample need, he argues, for Western Europeans to see the value of extending the civil space implied by such a security identity. Karp likewise argues that security needs exist, and must be addressed, but suggests less an extension of present institutions than the creation of new, far-reaching collective enterprises. Maynes' views concern what he sees as the failure of American policy to energize a global response to ethnic conflict. Miller addresses the role of the U.S. military in preventive diplomacy and other scenarios that would reinforce the security of fragile democracies and/or help to contain conflict.

One finds in all of these chapters a sense of the strenuous battle ahead against postauthoritarian disorder—a battle well worth fighting, if the goal is a regional or global system of stable democracies. Given that such an ideal will remain unachievable, we will need to reconfigure existing institutions, develop other collective organizations, adopt a vigorous diplomacy and the preventive use of U.S./multilateral military forces—all to provide whatever security we can.

For if democracy is, indeed, "security dependent," then we cannot expect insecure peoples and governments to maintain open, plural, and tolerant systems in the face of ominous perils. In threat-rich, capacity-poor states democratic change may rest precariously on an arrangement for externally provided security. And that challenge, in the view of these authors, is one from which Western democracies must not shrink.

Chapter 6

Refashioning Space and Security in Europe: Order versus Disorder

SIMON SERFATY

After the revolutions of 1989 in Europe—after authoritarianism—the United States and its allies acted quickly to refashion the institutional arrangements that had shaped their relations during the Cold War. From the London Declaration on a Transformed North Atlantic Alliance in July 1990 (when the Warsaw Pact ceased to be considered an immediate adversary) to the Rome Declaration on Peace and Cooperation in November 1991 (when the Western European Union ceased to be viewed as a potential rival), a multilayered security structure began to emerge: transatlantic with the North Atlantic Treaty Organization (NATO), pan-European with both a newly formed North Atlantic Cooperation Council (NACC) and an all-inclusive Conference on Security and Cooperation in Europe (CSCE), and *communautaire* with the European Community (EC) and a revitalized Western European Union (WEU). Together, these "interlocking institutions"—relying on the WEU as a temporary bridge—were expected to apply their respective assets and comparative advantages to promote cooperation with former adversaries, enhance economic recovery and political reform in the new democracies, balance responsibilities across the Atlantic, and deter conflict throughout a continent that would be made "whole and free" at last.

That such a creative momentum soon subsided ought not undermine the significance of such early initiatives.[1] Starting shortly after the Gulf War, an economic recession that was longer and more severe than expected ushered in a period of political volatility and social tensions in the West. In the United States, an increasingly exasperated public insisted that the victories recorded abroad could be achieved at home as well if only the new president gave as much attention to domestic issues as he gave to foreign issues. In Western Europe, conditions were reminiscent of those that had prevailed after the first oil crisis in late 1973, when political majorities were swept away in a matter of months and the EC was stalled for many years. Now, these new priorities, economic crises, and political changes shaped the divisions and passivity that characterized Western policies after the Cold War, especially in Yugoslavia, a conflict that also proved to be much more brutal and resilient than had been anticipated on either side of the Atlantic.

As the United States deplored once again a Europe that seemed unable to fulfill the promises of Maastricht, and as Europe feared once more a waning of the will for leadership which the United States had shown during the Gulf crisis, these new strains threatened the cohesion of the Western alliance. With the Soviet threat gone, how and where was European security at risk? With prospects for Europe's unity fading, how and when could the burden of the American commitment be shared? As U.S. troops stationed in Europe for nearly four decades were going home, by whom and how would the resulting vacuum be filled? Could NATO outlast the disappearance of a visible and dangerous Soviet threat, and would the process of European integration endure with a reunified and self-assured Germany— or would the dissolution of NATO and the stagnation of Europe's unification prove to be the price that the West had to pay for its "victory" in the Cold War?

That these questions were raised with mounting impatience or apprehension on both sides of the Atlantic reflected the doubts that had often surrounded U.S.-European relations in the past. After the authoritarianism of European communism, and the sense that democracy was emerging in many places, a logic of withdrawal seemed justified—an argument made many times before by critics who viewed the U.S. presence in Europe as detrimental to the interests it was expected to serve, whatever form this presence took and however these interests might be defined.[2] The Soviet collapse, the demise of communism, the liberation of Eastern Europe, the unification of Germany were all attributable to the resilience of the Western alliance. These events should have been heralded as good reasons for staying the course, and expanding eastward the common and civil space already built in the West. Instead, emphasis was placed on the many dangers which these achievements appeared to raise within and between the former Soviet republics, as well as the former members of the Warsaw Pact. Was disorder in the East the price countries in the region would have to pay for their defeat—with the down payment delivered in the former Yugoslavia? Or could a novel East-West bargain across Europe coupled with a modified West-West bargain across the Atlantic help contain, and even end, such disorder?

ORGANIZING THE WEST AFTER WORLD WAR II

After World War II the organization of the West was a multilateral and multidimensional undertaking that was neither conceptualized on the quick nor implemented on the cheap. For many years, there was no clear definition of the threat. Germany's status as a former enemy state caused passionate debate: did security in Europe demand the denial or the resurgence of German power? If the latter, could German power be trusted? If not, how would it be managed? Even the scope of Soviet intentions seemed vague. Beyond the traditional Russian drive for a sphere of influence in Central and southeastern Europe, including a determination to keep control of a part of Germany at least, how far west did Soviet ambitions extend, and what form did they take? Soviet military power was widely acknowledged to be ample, but Soviet leaders were not thought to be ready yet for another war. Accordingly, the threat of Soviet invasion from without (with likely support from internal forces) was found less serious at first than the risks of communist subversion from within (with a predictable assist from external forces). These risks, and the instabilities they caused, were deemed serious enough to justify an ever wider range of U.S. commitments enforced over a period of time. The most prominent of these commitments ranged from the economic (Marshall Plan) to the political (regional cooperation), and from the political (Washington Treaty) to the military (NATO).

Nor should the limits and the conditions initially placed on U.S. commitments be overlooked: the new allies were hardly offered a free ride. Thus, negotiating a finite amount of Marshall aid for economic recovery *and* political stability required a prior demonstration of the recipients' will for reconciliation and cooperation: hence the inclusion of Germany in the Organization for Economic Cooperation in Europe (OECE), which was devised not only to distribute the U.S. economic aid but also to act as a political conduit for reconciliation in Europe. Next, signing a guarantee pact—the 1949 Washington Treaty—for an explicit period of time required conclusive evidence of Europe's commitment to helping itself: that evidence was provided by the 1948 Brussels Pact, which created the embryo of a Western European Union (WEU) among France, Great Britain, and the three Benelux countries. And last, transforming the Western alliance into an integrated military coalition—namely, NATO—that would satisfy the requirements for collective defense written into Article V of the 1949 Treaty first demanded that the Soviet threat acquire a distinct military dimension. And, with events in 1948–1949 such as the Czech coup, the Berlin blockade, the Soviet A-bomb, and the communist victory in China, the urgency of the Soviet threat was made fully recognizable after the outbreak of the Korean War in 1950. Thus evolved the outlook of the Truman administration, the vision of which by the time it left office in January 1953 had changed markedly since it had been presented to Congress in the spring of 1947. Thus, too, was born a North Atlantic security area that "entangled" the United States in Europe more than had been anticipated because the allies proved to be too weak to be abandoned and the adversaries too strong to be ignored.[3]

But these first initiatives still failed to settle the status of the former enemy states, especially the Federal Republic of Germany. The U.S. insistence on including Germany as a beneficiary of, and participant in, all Western cooperative arrangements was not only military and economic but also, and even primarily, political: its ultimate goal was to prevent a resurgence of nationalism in the Federal Republic as well as throughout Western Europe. Visibly forced to drop the pretense of postwar unity in Europe in the face of a widening East-West divide, the Truman administration sought to ensure that there would not be more than two Europes, plus a few states whose neutrality did not alter the balance of forces on the continent. European requests for bilateral alliances with the United States were, therefore, mostly ignored.[4] Instead, the multilateral arrangements favored in Washington were designed to build new habits of cooperation among European states that would be made united enough to end old conflicts in the West and strong enough to help deter new ones with the East.

Jean Monnet was the European architect of this grand design. Yet the blueprint drafted by Monnet, and endorsed by enlightened European statesmen, became possible only when it was adopted by Truman and his administration. Only the United States could give the fiction *communautaire* in Europe the time and the space it needed to become a reality—time extended in the hope that economic recovery and political reconstruction might help forget past wars, and space expanded in the knowledge that America's unprecedented security commitments to the Old World would help balance a future renewal of Germany's political influence and even military power.

To this extent, if the Atlantic idea was a European concept designed to end a protracted historical detour that had kept America isolated from the continent, the concept of a united Europe was an American idea designed to cure a geographic accident that had kept Europe excessively fragmented.[5] Both ideas were separate: relying on different assets they aimed at different goals (mostly, though not exclusively, political security and economic recovery, respectively). But they could not be implemented separately. America's will to enter into an ever-closer alliance with the countries of Western Europe depended on their will to pursue an ever-closer union among themselves.

This is not to suggest that the United States never had any misgiving about the course of European unification and its impact on U.S. interests and leadership. As stability returned and affluence spread, continental calls for a narrow European community often clashed with America's preference for the broader Atlantic community that provided these states with security and confidence. It followed that transatlantic discord was common throughout the Cold War. Yet, none of the many crises that grew out of this discord was ever destructive of either the European identity the allies attempted to restore and preserve, or of the Atlantic personality the United States sought to foster and deepen. At worst, each Atlantic crisis might (or might be used to) exacerbate divisions in Europe, as happened during the formative years of the European Economic Community (EEC) following the disastrous Anglo-French intervention in Suez in 1956, with the quarrels that accompanied Britain's bid for EEC membership in the 1960s, during the monetary turbulence that preceded and followed the first oil crisis in the 1970s, and over the most effective ways to close a widening window of vulnerability in Europe in the early 1980s. In every instance, however, the Soviet threat was the glue that prevented the discord from going too far or lasting too long. In short, from crisis to crisis the identity of the European Community survived and penetrated further while the personality of the Atlantic community, too, endured and deepened.

Thus, although both the idea of Europe and the Atlantic idea were born out of the world wars, both drew strength and gained their rationale out of the Cold War.[6] Without Soviet hostility, America might have left Europe too quickly and Germany might have been reunified too soon since the weight of a unified Germany would have been too heavy for its frightened continental neighbors to begin a process of community building that required protection from without and balance from within. Moscow's alleged condition for the reunification of Germany was that it be kept out of the Western alliance. But neither neutrality nor disarmament was acceptable to the allies (or a majority of Germans) because the latter would have weak-ened the containment of Soviet power (America's primary concern) while the former would have also compromised the management of German power (Europe's initial priority).

After each superpower had sought to make the other responsible for the stalemate, the enlargement of NATO and the establishment of the Warsaw Pact Organization (WPO) in May 1955 institutionalized a territorial status quo that placed the Federal Republic firmly in the West—the place where it had been born because of war, and now the place where it could prosper in peace. As the division of its most dangerous adversary thus seemed irreversible, the need for Britain's presence on the continent as a counter-weight to Germany's influence ceased to be imperative. In 1957, therefore, France could accept, with the Rome Treaty, the small Europe *à six* that had been passionately rejected a few years earlier. But such a Europe now relied on a far more modest organizational device than before—an economic rather than a defense community, even though its central purpose remained unchanged—to lock Germany into the cage of regional unity. In short, the Cold War produced two Europes in which the two German states, inherited from two world wars, served the needs of the two superpowers and the aspirations of their respective allies on the continent.

FASHIONING A NEW EUROPE DURING THE COLD WAR

"How do you tell the present?" asked Dean Acheson in the midst of the war in Korea.[7] The end of the Cold War has brought back to life a European past that had been left for dead. The ghosts of its history are sighted from one Sarajevo to another, and from either Sarajevo to Simferopol. They carry with them the horror of genocide in southeastern Europe, the garbs of appeasement in the West, and the motion of national expansion in Eastern Europe.

The new Europe is not even born, and already it looks old and decrepit. Its past is widely viewed as its future. No imagination is required to describe it: what will be seems mostly to be whatever is remembered of the past, and what is remembered is mainly whatever is feared about the future. Shall we anticipate another imperial drive of Russia, beginning in Ukraine, where may lie the most urgent and most dangerous legacy of the Cold War? Ought we to expect another German bid for regional dominance—already achieved twenty years ago in the context of the European Community but now made possible in Central Europe as well?[8] And, is another global conflict starting in the Balkans—where a victorious Serbia might test Western passivity beyond the gains already achieved at the expense of Croatia and Bosnia-Herzegovina? Perhaps, too, should we prepare for another flurry of economic depression and political radicalism in the Western democracies—where the centrist republics built during the Cold War are exposed to renewed pressures from suddenly revived nationalist forces?

That the end of the Cold War era would generate new instabilities and uncertainties throughout the continent should have been expected: so it was after each world war. Yet the brutality unveiled during Yugoslavia's ethnic conflicts was all the more shocking as decades of economic prosperity in the West and of political calm in the East had widely encouraged a belief—a conviction—that Europe's murderous insanity had been cured at last. To this extent, no country on either side of the Atlantic was prepared to heed the warnings that accompanied the drift to war in what was still Yugoslavia at the time, when there might still have been time to prevent the tragedies that followed yet without enough time for a mental transition from the euphoria of peace to the hysteria of war. As images of violence were watched with increasing dismay and embarrassment, presenting them as preordained by the character of Slavic people and the region's history of hatred was not enough. Now, each ally delegated to its partners in Europe and across the Atlantic responsibility for actions it was unwilling to under-take itself—Europe's trial of post–Cold War unity (for the Europeans) or America's test of post–Cold War leadership.

Yet, however tragic the war in Bosnia was, it also served as an indicator of changes in Europe since the century began. In 1914, the mostly fortuitous assassination of an archduke in Sarajevo should have caused a relatively small conflict of imperial succession that might have killed, say, tens of thousands while it altered the geographic configuration of the region. Instead, it produced a global war that killed tens of millions while causing the historical collapse of the entire continent. In 1914, an increasingly affluent Europe had lived without a major war for nearly one hundred years, and this eruption of violence should have been viewed with dismay by states that had become used to peace. Instead, people everywhere welcomed the war almost enthusiastically, and the conflict spread dramatically. After the killing finally stopped in 1919, a moment of sanity might have been expected, among the victorious states as well as the defeated states. Instead, America and Europe returned to their old ways—an isolation that could no longer be sustained because no continental balance could be achieved between a *revanchiste* Germany and a revolutionary Russia.

Analogies between the "then of the pre- and interwar years" and the "now of the post–Cold War years" may be seductive.[9] They are not convincing, however. Europe's prewar will to fight has been exhausted, and its postwar wish to punish has been cured. Considering what happened over Sarajevo in 1914 the passivity shown in 1994 is not all bad news: at least, there could not be in 1994 the kind of escalation that had occurred in 1914, and the next worst alternative to "doing something" earlier still was the dreadful quagmire that might have resulted from doing something too early. And, considering the fate of the Weimar Republic, the accommodating spirit shown toward Russia also had its good points: at least Russia did not have to fear in 1994 the same outcome as there had been for Germany in 1918.

It is, of course, in Western Europe that the conditions of the past have most visibly changed. While history moved on, geography moved—which is to say that as the politicomilitary intensity of historical relations faded in Western Europe, its socioeconomic space was so altered as to transform the meaning of geographic conditions too.[10] Such geohistorical refashioning of space and time is especially dramatic with regard to France and a unified Germany, whose confrontation during the first half of the century produced one war per generation, and decimated one generation per war. Now, both countries have relations comparable in some aspects to those between the United States and Canada.

To be sure, economic rivalries, political suspicions, and even national rancor still exist. A *ménage à trois* between the EU's main powers remains elusive. Prior to World War I, France and Germany vied for Britain's support: even the Entente Cordiale did not end the competition, as doubts about the reliability of the entente lingered in Paris as well as in Berlin. Prior to World War II, the Anglo-French alliance was not in question but its significance was: appeasement was welcome in both countries. After World War II, France sought out Britain's help against Germany. Later, however, France and Germany began to act in unison without, or after 1973 mostly in spite of, Britain.

But for these countries, as well as for the other imperial performers of the past (including Belgium, Holland, and Portugal, as well as Austria), war has ceased to be thinkable. Now, instead, they are grouped into a "community" where the individual "I" of each nation-state influences, and is influenced by, a collective "We" that includes a finite but never final number of member states—from six to nine, ten or twelve; and from twelve to fifteen and more. In short, the little secret uncovered during Europe's multispeed history of false starts is that it is no longer enough for the states of Europe to limit their identity and their security to the nation. They have to be something more—which is the new reality *communautaire* of Europe: namely, an executive (the Commission) without a government, a government (the Council) without a country, and a country (the Community) without an identity. Therein lies the most tangible legacy of the history that shaped the Cold War, as well as the most identifiable change from the geography that produced the previous two world wars.

Admittedly, taking this new Europe seriously remains daunting. Throughout the Cold War, the EC performed as an institutional underachiever whose timetables were ignored, delayed, or abandoned when they ceased to satisfy the goals and interests of all EU members. Pointedly enough, the timetables that proved to be the most reliable had to do only with trade issues—a common market first, and a single market next—in the context of agreements that did not seem to be taken seriously by their most serious proponent (the Rome Treaty and France in 1957) or opponent (the Single European Act and Great Britain in 1987).[11] Predictably enough, agreements that proved to be most controversial involved schemes of political union which EC states were still unprepared to accept after the 1991 Maastricht Treaty exaggerated the momentum gained by the orderly organization of the single market and which were effectively derailed by the debates that surrounded its dismissal in 1993 and 1994.

Thus, if emphasis is placed on the limits of political union, or on the unfinished business of economic and monetary union, the EC looms like an institutional failure that compares poorly with other Western institutions, especially NATO. Yet beyond the stillborn plans that formulated the broad alphabet of Europe's failures, the history of "Europe" teaches that no setback was irreversible, no obstacle proved to be insurmountable, and no voice of dissent remained unforgettable.[12] The evidence of failure is found day-to-day, but the symptoms of progress are uncovered over time: the evidence, that is, that after each crisis has reassured those who fear that Europe is moving too fast and too broadly, there is always a reliance that reassures those who fear that Europe is moving too slowly and too timidly.

REFASHIONING THE WEST FOR A COLD PEACE

"People [in Europe]," noted Dean Acheson in early 1950, "are questioning whether [the North Atlantic Treaty] really means anything, since it means only what we are able to do. Our intentions are not doubted, but our capabilities are."[13] At the time, the Washington Treaty had barely been signed, NATO had not been organized, and the Cold War had barely started. More than forty years later, the Western alliance is still based mostly on the

United States: what it remains willing to do, and how much it is willing to contribute now that the East-West confrontation is over. Yet while U.S. capabilities no longer seem to be questioned in Europe (only its intentions), the allies' intentions and capabilities both remain seriously questioned in the United States. In an atmosphere of disarray exacerbated but not caused by the war in Bosnia, NATO and the EU—the EC was renamed European Union (EU) in late 1993—risk becoming out-of-date unless they deepen their links with each other, and widen their membership to others.

That the North Atlantic Treaty and its organization would remain the central feature of European security is hardly an ideal situation. In an ideal setting, the Cold War would have ended with a strong and united European community ready for, and capable of, self-help in a continent made at last peaceful. Regrettably, this is not the case. Events in Bosnia and elsewhere, and instabilities in Russia and in the former Soviet republics, show that pretending otherwise may be not only illusory but even dangerous. For now as before, there can be no effective European action without an active American participation, whether to make peace or keep it, whether militarily or politically.[14]

Refashioning the West after the demise of its authoriarian adversaries starts, therefore, with the same premise as fashioning the West after World War II: the premise of a continued U.S. commitment to Europe so long as the promise of its unification has not been totally fulfilled. Why this commitment would be extended beyond the nearly five decades it took to end the Cold War, and how it would be sustained without the 300,000 American troops whose deployment has been a fixture of Europe's security for nearly three decades, is no more self-evident now than the extension of that commitment and the decision for such deployment were after World War II.

But leaving Europe is no longer the option it was once (or twice) upon a time; and being in Europe no longer carries the same connotation as it did in the past. For now, America's identity as a European power is shaped by the "new maths" of an American presence that transcends the military arithmetic of the past. Thus, thirty-seven years after the 1957 Rome Treaty was questioned for its protectionist culture, economic ties across the Atlantic define a space whose unity nearly parallels the unity of space achieved in the European community. In this common space, each side buys from, sells to, and invests and produces in, the other—at a pace that exceeds an estimated $1,000 billion each year (including trade and the output of U.S.- and European-owned companies in Europe and the United States). In this common space where the United States is a state within the community,

American firms that have invested about $240 billion in the EU are accepted as the leading European firms they have become even as they struggle as the American corporate giants they have remained (with about two-fifths of all U.S. profits earned abroad deriving from Western Europe).

These interests are hardly negligible. They confirm that over the years and from either side of the Atlantic, the ocean has been bridged: over there is now over here (and, admittedly, is, or may expand to, nearly everywhere).

This is perhaps the most striking outcome of the vision that animated America's policies during the Cold War: its rise as a European power reflects interests without which it might be difficult to imagine—let alone endure—life. In 1919 the invitation to stay could be ignored, and it was. In 1945 withdrawal remained an option, but it was ignored. Now, the option is gone and the invitation no longer needs to be extended. What remains, instead, is a European and transatlantic space that bears little resemblance to what it was before but can no longer become again.

At least twelve of the states of Europe, and the United States with them, have been locked into a cage with one another for which no one occupant appears to have the key anymore. Once upon a time, France used it to keep Germany in, and the countries of the East out. But in the early 1970s Germany seized that key, and twenty years later the German government hopes to use it to open the doors *communautaires* to the former adversaries in the East. Meanwhile, no member state is anxious to leave and most nonmember states remain anxious to join. The same is true of the Atlantic cage too. Formerly, America held the key to keep members in (and the East out). Now, the door seems to be locked mostly to keep nonmembers out, although some basic facilities are made available for rental. These are the Partnership for Peace options, which every state in the East is said to be willing to consider, even though none appears quite willing to applaud.

There is, of course, little doubt that NATO and EU expansion will occur, however slowly. As they do, they will transform the patterns of intra-European and transatlantic relations, just as the organization of NATO and the launching of EC did more than forty years ago. On the western side of the continent, but also with North America, the common security space fashioned by history must be defended in common. To argue the end of NATO is to argue the end of war or the birth of Europe. At best, both ideas are premature. As the only superpower left on the continent, NATO is bound to play the security role it played under different circumstances during the Cold War. Who else? Only NATO has the capabilities, training, and experience for such leadership. The case for the Western European Union is not argued in opposition but in addition to that for NATO. As the only existing defense organization that gathers together the main EU countries, the WEU can be the European pillar of NATO. At the same time, the WEU can rely on NATO infrastructure assets for EU action in or out of the NATO area without, but not in spite of, the United States. In short, the reform of NATO, which has to do with how much (less) the United States will continue to ˜contribute, is linked to the completion of Europe (including WEU); while the completion of Europe, which has to do with how much (more) the Europeans will begin to provide, remains tied to the preservation of NATO.

But that transatlantic space must also acknowledge the geographic imperatives it faces on a European continent that may be more free than before but still remains divided. Admittedly, NATO with sixteen members—plus the new partners gathered together according to needs, capabilities, and traditions—may well fulfill the security functions that have already emerged, and are likely to continue to emerge, from the Cold War. But NATO does not have comparable influence and resources for attending to the economic dimensions of security about which it can only play a supportive role. This role belongs more specifically to the EU. In a European space that is no longer divisible but still remains divided, the form and pace of disintegration in the East affect the substance of integration in the West. Poverty and affluence do not coexist any more peacefully in that civil and militarized space. Failure to bridge this division would perpetuate the historic error which the countries of Europe have often attributed to the Yalta agreement, while failing to ensure that new authoritarians will not have economic nutrients with which to feed a renewed attack on democracies.

In short, the West cannot escape the need to share its strength with, and extend its unity to, the East: separately because its central institutions (NATO and the EU) cater to different needs, and yet together because these needs (security and recovery) are complementary and cannot be satisfied separately.

THE LIGHT AT THE END OF THE TUNNEL

Any phase of multiple transitions comparable to that which has been lived, however briefly, since the end of the Cold War reinforces the desirability of defining an end point that might give coherence to the changes that are unfolding. As George Kennan once put it, a "lantern" is needed to illuminate "a bit of the path ahead" and "a bit of the path behind"—the proverbial light at the end of the tunnel. Yet the relevance of that light cannot be overstated. What is illuminated remains a moving target, now clear and visible, now blurred and elusive.

A century that opened with the excitement of an allegedly *belle époque*, when it was said to be "a good time to be alive," closes with the uncertainties anchored in the insanities that brought the world to the brink of oblivion with two global wars, and nearly forced people all over the world into submission with two insane utopias—fascism and Communism. Yet, there is enough that lurches through these uncertainties to reassure and make the observer hope that the cause that was just during each desperate but passing moment kept the course hopeful and ultimately right.

"A constructive treatment of Europe's present-day problems," wrote Hajo Holborn shortly after World War II, "calls for historical thinking which is something more than mere historical knowledge."[15] Historical thinking requires a will to see beyond the detours taken in the fleeting present. Admittedly, the present inherited from the Cold War has left both sides of the Atlantic—and both sides of Europe—with much cause for despondency. Order has not come as easily as had been hoped. Uncertainties abound, and instabilities threaten everywhere. But gloom has lost much of the appeal it may have had because it proved to be exaggerated so many times in the past. As the wall in Berlin came down, and communism collapsed, and democratic reforms began in the East at a pace that left little room for imagination, changes did not run out of control. They only added a few milestones on the long journey toward a more orderly and more satisfying future. This future will come: less painfully than used to be the case although not as rapidly as was hoped to be the case.

NOTES

1. A version of this chapter appears in Michael Brenner, ed., *Multilateralism and Western Strategy* (London: Macmillan, 1995); New York: St. Martin's Press, 199), with the kind permission of both publishers.

2. During the Cold War, calls for a U.S. troop withdrawal from Europe were made on diverse grounds. But such a withdrawal was almost always viewed as the most effective way to make the allies do more on their own behalf. Standing in the way of this "logic" was the risk that a premature U.S. withdrawal might cause a *sauve-qui-peut* that would expose Europe (and U.S. interests in Europe) to Soviet power and influence. With the Cold War over, the demise of Soviet power could now be said to permit a test of this logic at no cost.

3. These postwar decisions were not easy. In Europe, reconciliation with Germany was a steep price to pay for U.S. support. In the United States, a peacetime alliance outside the Western Hemisphere was a drastic diplomatic step.

With the benefit of hindsight, what impresses most is the quality of the leadership which, on both sides of the Atlantic, insisted on, and acquiesced to, the conditions that shaped these decisions.

4. John Gerard Ruggie, "Multilateralism: The Anatomy of an Institution," *International Organization* (Summer 1992): 588.

5. These themes are developed at greater length in the author's *Taking Europe Seriously* (New York: St. Martin's Press, 1992).

6. Simon Serfaty, "Odd Couples," in Gustav Schmidt, ed., *Ost-West Beziehungen*, 1 (Bochum: Brockmeyer, 1993), 73–82.

7. Dean Acheson, "What Is the Present, What Is the Future," *The New York Times Magazine* (June 22, 1952).

8. Zbigniew Brzezinski, "The Premature Partnership," *Foreign Affairs* (March–April 1994): 67–82; Connor Cruise O'Brien, "The Future of the West," *National Interest* (Winter 1992/93): 3–10. Also, Simon Serfaty, "The Challenge of Continuity: Hyperboles, Hysteria and History," in Jeff Simon, ed., *NATO: The Challenge of Change* (Washington, D.C.: National Defense University Press, 1993), 21–37.

9. Richard E. Neustadt and Ernest R. May, *Thinking in Time: The Use of History for Decision Makers* (New York: Free Press, 1986), 66.

10. Peter J. Taylor, *Britain and the Cold War: 1945 as a Geopolitical Transition* (New York: Guilford Press, 1990), 10.

11. In 1957, skeptics included Jean Monnet, for whom the "ever closer union" sought by the Rome Treaty was "rather vague." From his self-imposed political exile, General de Gaulle did not hide his contempt for a treaty which he reportedly planned to discard at the first opportunity. That de Gaulle presided nonetheless over the implementation of the treaty in the 1960s was a change of mind rather than a change of heart: the Common Market worked better than even its proponents had anticipated. In 1984–1987, Prime Minister Thatcher misunderstood the evolution of the European Community. "Looking back," she writes, "I see the period somewhat differently. . . . It was only in my last days in office . . . that the true scale of the challenge [raised by the Community's goal] has become clear." Margaret Thatcher, *The Downing Street Years* (New York: HarperCollins, 1993), 536.

12. See the author's "Commitment without Purpose," in Michael Clark and S. Serfaty, eds., *Old Thinking and New Reality* (Washington, D.C.: Seven Locks Press, 1991), 127–161.

13. Quoted in Jack Snyder, *Myths of Empire: Domestic Politics and International Ambitions* (Ithaca, N.Y.: Cornell University Press, 1991), 260.

14. Admittedly, the reverse was true: American intervention depended on active participation by the European allies, thereby reinforcing either side's ability to justify its passivity in terms of the other's unwillingness to make a sufficient contribution to the common effort.

15. Hajo Holborn, *The Collapse of Europe* (New York: Alfred A. Knopf, 1951), xi.

Chapter 7

Postcommunist Europe: Back from the Abyss?

REGINA KARP

THE FADING HOPE OF A NEW ORDER

With the end of the Cold War, hopes of shaping a peaceful European security order abounded. History had given Europe the chance to re-create itself, as a continent of democracies, from states cast aside by decades of division and ideological struggle. Although these hopes have not been abandoned, it is increasingly obvious that they will not be realized in the near future. Much more likely in the short and medium term is a European security order that cannot easily be defined as either peaceful or conflictual.

The European continent is in the midst of geopolitical upheaval, the direction, pace, and outcome of which are as yet only partially comprehensible. The nature of this upheaval is better understood than its ultimate course. In essence, the transformation of Europe goes to the heart of post–cold War international relations, raising basic questions about nations and states, domestic reform and regional stability, the sources of conflict, and the role of international organizations in the prevention and settlement of disputes.[1]

For Cold War Europe, these questions were moot. The stark divisions between East and West and membership in respective alliances provided a previously unparalleled degree of strategic certainty: alliances provided hierarchy, leadership, and identity. Consensus existed about both the enemy's identity and about what threats would trigger alliance and national defense efforts. The threat that each alliance perceived as emanating from the other provided sufficient cohesion for intra-alliance consensus and helped on many occasions to reconcile differences between member states over strategy and defense budgets. In sum, Cold War divisions made for an unusually predictable environment conducive to long-term military and political planning. Alliance members knew what was expected of them, accepted their responsibilities, and were confident about their joint ability to maintain security.

The end of the Cold War changed every aspect of the European security order taken for granted by politicians and academic analysts. The disintegration of the Soviet empire in Eastern Europe and the subsequent breakup of the Soviet Union itself, the unification of Germany, and the emergence of new states have caused a dramatic alteration of the conditions within which European security has to be created. The Cold War security framework is gone forever and with it the certainty of its institutional arrangements and patterns of interstate relations.

While it is recognized throughout Europe that traditional approaches to security no longer provide answers to new security problems, little progress toward a new security order has been made since 1989. Even more disturbing is the continued absence of a consensus able to guide steps toward a new security order. While political change as far-reaching as that experienced at the end of the Cold War takes time to be incorporated into policy, this explanation is already loosing credibility and is fast turning into an excuse for inaction. There is no agreement within and among Western European and Atlantic organizations on how the end of the Cold War translates into new political responsibilities or how it affects the future tasks of existing security institutions. Instead, there is a pervasive sense of disorientation as to what the immediate security issues are, who should deal with them, and who should lead the overall effort of building a new European order. Measures taken in response to pleas by Central and Eastern Europe to partake in Western organizations appear to have been aimed at defusing their political urgency rather than addressing them as part of an overall strategy for security building. The creation of the North Atlantic Cooperation Council (NACC), the expansion of membership in the Conference on Security and Cooperation in Europe in 1992, and NATO's offer of a Partnership for Peace have all been about making Western organizations appear less of a closed shop without making decisive commitments to Central and Eastern Europe. The exclusiveness of Western organizations has been maintained and the issue of membership fudged.[2]

The lack of a coherent approach to European security has been most starkly exposed over the war in Bosnia. In light of Western acquiescence to Serbian territorial ambitions, references to a new European order based on principles of liberal democracy ring hollow at best. At worst, they suggest a growing divide separating a secure and prosperous European West from an unstable and economically weak East. Western credibility has been severely compromised and its leadership role in creating a new European security order made doubtful. The end of the Cold War has not eliminated the use of force in Europe, and Western governments have to ask themselves if the new European order is to be shaped by promising a better and more prosperous future or by thwarting aggression when it so blatantly defies the principles and aspirations of the 1990 Charter of Paris. The West's failure to underpin diplomatic efforts at resolving the Bosnian war coupled with its unwillingness to use force does not promise greater decisiveness in the future.[3]

What the West can and is willing to contribute to the security of Central and Eastern Europe will determine much of the quality of security in the region. States in the region are newly independent actors, undergoing far-reaching processes of domestic restructuring. Their foreign policies are often haphazardly formulated, and coherent defense policies have yet to emerge. Struggles over foreign policy orientation display a polarization of domestic politics and the prevalence of continuing power struggles. After years of Soviet domination, states in the region have to establish domestic legitimacy and a foreign policy identity. These are difficult tasks, not least because they have to be undertaken against a backdrop of the deeply entrenched legacies of the communist era. Inevitably, though, governments have to make decisions on domestic reforms and foreign policy. Individual differences not withstanding, Central and Eastern European states share a historical experience of communist rule and its authoritarian political and economic structures. Even after the overthrow of communist governments, residual features of communism such as the lack of democratic institutions and the dislocation of economic resources hamper effective reform. The measures states have taken individually and collectively to overcome this legacy and to avert destabilizing social tensions highlight the grave political strains governments in the region are faced with.

The existence of a common legacy is also reflected in national efforts to devise security policies, create armed forces that meet the demands of the new security environment, and establish democratically accountable security institutions. These are formidable tasks demanding careful diplomacy *vis-à-vis* both domestic interests and neighboring states. Without exception,

Central and Eastern European countries have so far espoused only rudimentary defense doctrines and national security priorities. They are still in the process of understanding their new environment and distinguishing between immediate and longer-term security concerns. Most acutely, there is a pervading sense of security adrift, and a situation in which the uncertainty of domestic developments and regional fluidity are themselves seen as threatening.

A third commonality stems from the region-wide effort to overcome security uncertainty. States are inherently opposed to uncertainty in their relations with others. However, given the anarchic nature of the international system, it is up to states themselves to create a predictable environment and reduce uncertainty to a minimum. Failure to do so carries high risks. Conflicts are likely to emerge and the very existence of states may be threatened. In turn, these conflicts may lead to more uncertainty. One need not be an international relations theorist to recognize the futility of such a spiraling "security dilemma." The key question remains one of how to find ways to overcome systemic uncertainty.[4]

Postcommunist Central and Eastern Europe is rife with conflict. As peaceful as the overthrow of communism has been, it has left deep fissures. It has resulted in the creation of fifteen newly independent states, all formerly integral parts of the Soviet Union. Bereft of the unifying bond of communist government, many of these states have little to unite them. Different pre-Soviet histories, ethnic, cultural, and religious divisions are all acting to separate them. Their security needs are fiercely debated domestically and closely tied to debates about national identity. Volatile domestic politics make it difficult to find a consensus over national interests that can be clearly and reliably communicated. Consequently, countries send confusing signals about their security and foreign policy interests. This has particularly been the case regarding Russia and Ukraine, where relations have been plagued by power struggles between executive and legislative authorities. The inability of each country to resolve strictly domestic problems has aggravated relations with the other and decreased the security of both. Domestic power struggles have a direct impact upon foreign policy behavior, and while these continue, a country's external orientation remains unpredictable.

Ethnic and religious diversity add to domestic instability. Centuries of Ottoman, Habsburg, and, more recently, Soviet domination have left a geopolitical patchwork of arbitrarily drawn borders and nations divided. Many Central and Eastern European states have sizeable minorities within their borders: twenty-five million Russians alone currently are living outside Russia. Much depends on how a state treats its ethnic minorities. Whenever one state has cause to be concerned about the civil and human rights of its ethnic kin living in another, nationalist forces are likely to exploit these concerns. Though not as conflictual as the situation in the former Yugoslavia, the ethnic mix in many parts of Eastern Europe and the Balkans suggests that the issue of ethnicity has the potential to develop rapidly into a security problem of the first order. In several places war has already broken out either directly because of unreconcilable ethnic differences or because ethnicity is being exploited by one faction or another for its own political purposes. Most often there is an indistinguishable mix of ethnic and political causes; the wars in the former Yugoslavia, in Armenia and Azerbaijan, in the Trans-Dniester region of Moldova, in Abkhazia, and in South Ossetia are cases in point.

The threat of existing states breaking apart has already become reality in the former Yugoslavia and may become reality elsewhere. Though the divorce between the Czech and Slovak republics has been peaceful, the viability of the relatively poor and backward Slovak state is not yet assured. The Czechoslovak example should not, therefore, be taken as a model. Central and Eastern Europe are filled with claims to nation- and statehood— claims that often reflect a lack of understanding of the conditions that make for a viable state beyond ethnicity criteria.

This is an especially acute problem for Russia, where the threat of disintegration is worsening. While Russia's size and geopolitical location make it a prominent actor, more than seventy years of communist rule have left it almost paralyzed. Persistent constitutional deadlock between Parliament and the presidency over who can legitimately speak for the people has hampered necessary reforms, fragmented political will, and alienated the regions from the center. Reforms at all levels of political life are desperately needed. While no one expects large-scale reforms to be noncontroversial, it is the continued lack of visible reform progress that is socially destabilizing and, increasingly, politically unacceptable. Should reforms fail in Russia, it may be impossible to avert the breakup of the Russian Federation. In light of existing ethnic and border/territorial problems in Russia, there can be little doubt that such a development would be accompanied by major instabilities.

Russian parliamentary elections in December and the adoption of a new constitution, though envisaged to break the constitutional deadlock and enhance the powers of the presidency, have achieved neither. Russian reformers fared miserably in the elections, in part because they failed to pool their resources. Perhaps to a more considerable extent they failed

because the reform process had yielded more economic and social dislocation than improved living standards. Attributing economic hardship solely
to the professional shortcomings of the reformers themselves is misleading.
True, there have been many different plans to reform the Russian economy.
But none of these plans has been implemented in a coherent fashion.
Reforms cannot be undertaken under threats of hyper inflation, nor can
industrial performance be subject to market forces as long as huge state
subsidies distort the relationship between productivity and prices. By early
1994, the last of the reformers had left government.[5]

Unexpected winners of the December elections were the Liberal Democrats, who represent an unholy alliance of ultranationalists and a disaffected
populace. Though Vladimir Zhirinovsky may represent the extreme within
his own party, there is sufficient cause for concern that the forces that gave
rise to him might be here to stay unless and until the lot of the average
Russian improves. Paradoxically, this will make real reforms more difficult
and increase incentives for appeasing the nationalists by slowing down or
delaying necessary reforms. If the government opts for the latter, the
conditions for a political consensus able to see incisive reforms through
may not emerge.

Taken together, the intricate problems of economic and political transformation at the domestic level and their coupling with region-wide problems of overcoming outdated communist structures, ethnic diversity, and
age-old disputes over territory present a complex security picture. States in
the region have taken a variety of measures to reduce uncertainty in their
dealings with each other, to strengthen cooperation where possible, and to
defuse conflict should it arise. At the subregional level, the creation of
cooperative facilities and bodies such as (a) the Visegrad Group, consisting
of the Czech Republic, Hungary, Poland, and Slovakia; (b) the Central
European Initiative (CEI), comprising Austria, Bosnia and Herzegovina,
Croatia, the Czech Republic, Slovakia, and Slovenia; (c) the Baltic States
Council, consisting of Denmark, Estonia, Finland, Latvia, Lithuania, Germany, Norway, Poland, Russia, and Sweden; and (d) the Commonwealth
of Independent States (CIS), embracing a majority of post-Soviet states, are
all aimed at introducing a measure of cohesion into an otherwise diverse
environment. None of them, however, can or ever were intended to substitute for a subregional or region-wide security structure. Rather, they are
transient structures, identifying subregional commonalities and translating
them into cooperative initiatives.

While these efforts have achieved a modicum of success and are encouraged by Western Europe and the United States, in Central and Eastern

Europe they are clearly seen as secondary to achieving membership in both NATO and the European Union (EU). Since the end of the Cold War, this aim has been the most consistent foreign policy goal among the former Warsaw Treaty Organization (WTO) states. A series of motives underpin this strategic goal.

1. NATO and the European Union are viewed as functioning organizations. Among all the organizations begun in the Cold War era, it is these two that hold the greatest promise for European security and economic integration. Despite the problems faced by both NATO and the EU, Central and Eastern Europeans view them primarily in terms of what they have achieved rather than for what they might or might not evolve into. Past success is what inspires the desire to join, not an uncertain future.

2. To many of the Central and Eastern European states, especially those with historical links to the West, NATO and the European Union constitute the embodiment of liberal democratic values. Membership in these organizations is thus seen not only as furthering their external interests of security and integration but as vital for attaining and maintaining internal democracy. Thus understood, membership would anchor these newly independent states in communities which embody values they aspire to realize. To be an integral part of the West, and to finally dispel any notions of being anything else but Western, is what matters most.

3. Membership is identified as the only viable course by which to balance the might of Russia. There is little that is feared more than the specter of once again falling into Moscow's orbit. It is feared that if democratic and economic reforms fail, if Western markets are not opened up, and if the security situation in the region deteriorates, Russia may be tempted to assume the role of regional *Ordnungsmacht* (via the CIS or directly). Such a development would, in the eyes of many, nullify the gains brought about by the end of the Cold War. While currently confined to the "near abroad," the new assertiveness of Russian foreign policy reverberates beyond the boundaries of the former Soviet Union.[6]

4. Membership is sought because states feel that they are unable to solve their domestic and external problems by themselves. The actual or potential revival of the historical animosities which the region has never been able to handle motivates much of the desire to seek external help. Each nation wants to anchor the state in structures that appear to have overcome conflict between states. The example of Franco-German reconciliation and the envelopment of German power within multilateral structures of integration is not lost on Central and Eastern European governments.

5. Central European countries fear that, absent prompt membership in NATO and the EU, they will return to their traditional role as buffers between East and West. This would place them in a security "no-man's-land" in which they would be neither within the Russian orbit nor close to the West. Such marginalization, it is feared, would leave Central and Eastern European states in perpetual uncertainty, in limbo between potential Russian ambition and Western neglect.

The Western response to these demands for institutional membership has not been encouraging. While the door to eventual membership in NATO and the EU remains open, the path to this goal is far from straightforward. In the case of the EU, there are conditions on economic performance and democratic development that must be met. In the case of NATO, the alliance has proved reluctant to accept an eastward expansion of its membership. Thus, almost four years after the end of the Cold War, Europe has not managed to overcome its erstwhile division, and the hopes espoused in the 1990 Charter of Paris for a New Europe have remained unfulfilled.

How could security for all Europe be achieved? How could Western Europe's prosperity and security be extended to foster democratic developments and dispel insecurity in the East? Western governments are aware of the profound insecurity that exists on the territory of the former WTO. They are aware that, without Western engagement, the chances of creating a security structure for the continent are slim. There are few signs that the countries of Central and Eastern Europe can manage the transition to democracy on their own. We are fully aware that the gravity of the situation has made Western responses appear puny. Effects of ending the Cold War have been, it seems, as profound on the Western political psyche as they have been on the former WTO.

Throughout the Cold War era, NATO provided security against a threat *from* the East. NATO plans and NATO resources were all geared toward safeguarding its members against potential WTO aggression. Two generations of politicians and defense bureaucrats were socialized into thinking of European security in terms of Western or Atlantic security. The issues of security were intimately familiar; they revolved around the alliance's strategy of flexible response, defense procurement options, debates about the nuclear threshold, and the role of nuclear weapons in Europe generally. For Western governments it was clear what a *European* contingency was: an attack by the East. None of this comfortable simplicity has remained.

In place of this once familiar scenario, Western countries are confronted with a perplexing picture. On the one hand, their own physical security has never been more assured. Germany, for example, is surrounded by friends for the first time since Charlemagne. Further, none of Germany's neighbors have the remotest desire or military capacity to pose a strategic threat. Although nuclear weapons remain a concern, their relevance to Western security is greatly diminished. On the other hand, new threats have emerged. These are not threats to the physical security of Western Europe but, instead, threats to the quality of security in Europe as a whole.

When the Cold War ended, all existing barriers that had kept the two parts of Europe apart were removed. Europe became *de facto* a united continent. In this sense, there can be no partial security; it is either for all or for no one, and is indivisible. The war in the former Yugoslavia demonstrates clearly that conflict in Europe is a collective burden, and that its occurrence, and the feeble responses to it, make a profound statement about the quality of security in Europe. This quality is far from uniform. Indeed, security appears to be European only in the sense that it *happens* on the European continent or to the extent that it can claim to involve the security of the member states of the Organization on Security and Cooperation in Europe (OSCE). Neither established security relationships between states nor security structures that integrate Europe to make it a single security space exist. For whom security is offered and guaranteed remains to be established.

Western governments continue to take a myopic view of what is relevant to their security while the conflict potential *within* Central and Eastern Europe grows. As a consequence, Europe's need for a unifying security framework is ever more urgent but also increasingly more daunting. In order to act creatively, Western governments need first to understand the implications of political change in Europe and make this understanding an essential part of their approach to security policy. This requirement has three elements:

1. There is a need to recognize that the primary questions of European security no longer revolve around stable military balances but around stable political relationships. For the fledgling democracies in Central and Eastern Europe this is true at the domestic and external levels. Stable domestic relationships encompass political consensus on national identity, democratization of political and economic processes, accepted divisions of executive and legislative authority, and respect for human rights. External stability stands for a rejection of the use of force in the settlement of disputes. None of these conditions is assured.

2. Western governments must understand the synergistic relationship between internal and external stability. Democracy is unlikely to flourish under conditions of external threat. Equally, external security cannot be

assumed to emerge from among states with volatile domestic politics. Thus both aspects of stability need to be pursued together and political strategies to that effect have to be developed.

3. The West needs to recognize just how important the future of Central and Eastern Europe is to its own interests. Western Europe cannot afford to concentrate exclusively on the problem of its own integration while ignoring the need to integrate the Central and Eastern European nations. A Europe divided between rich and poor, between secure and insecure states, is not a viable security option. Separation, as practiced during the Cold War era, must not become the model for post–Cold War relations. Instead, processes of integration should be strengthened. Many in the EU, however, worry that a widening of membership would slow progress or even endanger the move toward a European Union. This concern, however justified, is not an answer to the question of how integration in Europe should proceed.

The EU needs to both widen and deepen simultaneously. Democratization and security building in Central and Eastern Europe is only possible if Western integration succeeds. Unless the EU proceeds with its plans for political union, plans which entail a commitment to joint foreign and defense policy making, it will not be able to address the economic, political, and security issues troubling Europe. Without the diplomatic and military tools that only a European Union can offer, the EU will become marginalized on its own doorstep. If the EU wants to avoid this fate, it will have to become stronger and more relevant to the problems that plague Europe at present. Becoming stronger means that the EU has to be seen as still committed to a union; becoming more relevant means that it has to extend the promise of membership not only to those countries that appear to have overcome the worst, like the Czech Republic, Hungary, and Poland, but to those who are in greatest need. In the new political environment, the EU must cease to regard itself as a club of relatively successful market democracies and recognize that its own relevance depends vitally on recognizing the pivotal political role it can and must play in furthering stability in all of Europe.

The processes of political change thus have a profound effect on both Central and Eastern Europe and the West. For the countries of Central and Eastern Europe, economic and political circumstances make integration with the West the only alternative to domestic and regional instability. For the West, there is no choice between widening and deepening. All its ambitions for a union and its credibility as an international actor are tied to the future of Central and Eastern Europe. The tools for tackling present conflicts will become available only through the furtherance of the project of a European Union. Without the countries of Central and Eastern Europe, however, such a union will be meaningless.

QUO VADIS, SECURITY?

For Europe, the challenge is to move from the shattered remains of the Cold War era security system toward a new security order. Five principal options present themselves. Each has its own strengths and weaknesses, all of which need to be assessed carefully. Moreover, an evaluation of these options must be based on an assessment of the current and future security needs on the continent. What makes this evaluation difficult is the sheer complexity of the present security picture. What, indeed, would an appropriate security system be? What would be its responsibilities and how should these responsibilities be executed?

The *first* security option envisages the emergence of new alliances balancing one another and thus keeping the peace. Each alliance would be led by a major power that would determine its security orientation. Reminiscent of Cold War era alliances, this security system also displays the same weaknesses as the old order. Alliances are about the separation of security needs. They assume that states can be grouped according to clearly differing security presumptions and that these will be maintained over time. Adopting such a structure for Europe would mean that the assumption of "security separateness" still holds true and that there are still clearly differing security needs among countries. In reality, neither assumption is valid. Europe is separated today not by different security ideologies but by unequal security. A system of alliances would perpetuate security separateness despite the absence of any identifiable foe or any ideological division between identifiable blocs.

For Central and Eastern European countries, an alliance arrangement would almost certainly mean closer association with Russia. This would enhance Russia's geopolitical position since there can be little doubt that Russia would dominate an eastern alliance. It is doubtful, however, whether Russia would be capable of such leadership either at present or in the foreseeable future. Uncertain domestic politics and the ultimate fate of the Russian Federation itself impede Russia's ability to lead. Russia would thus be dominating an alliance through its weaknesses rather than its strengths, a virtual prescription for instability. Even if Russian democratic reforms were to proceed at greater pace, memories of the excesses of Russian and Soviet domination are still too vivid to permit voluntary Central and Eastern European association around Russia.

For the West, an alliance would mean maintaining NATO in much of its current form and size. Despite the loss of its traditional *raison d'être* caused by the breakup of the Soviet Union and the disappearance of the WTO, NATO has nevertheless shown remarkable resilience. It does, however, face major problems. For one, in order to retain its position as Europe's primary security organization, it needs to be seen tackling Europe's foremost security problems successfully. Thus far, NATO has not shown itself to be up to the task. The debacle over its handling of the war in former Yugoslavia, especially with respect to if and when and how and for what purpose to intervene militarily, has exposed deep fissures among member states concerning the alliance's role and responsibilities in Europe. Clearly, NATO needs to evolve. As a classic alliance it has no future in a security environment in which there is no permanent strategic threat but rather a myriad of complex and often messy instabilities. Alliances do not appear to offer promising paths toward building security in Europe. Inherently divisive, they are unable to build upon the gains of the end of the Cold War. Instead, they perpetuate the security conditions of a bygone era.

A *second* option deserving consideration when discussing how security in Europe should be built concerns the "renationalization" of security. It is based on the assumption that in the absence of the familiar threat from the East, NATO cannot survive indefinitely if it is unable to carve out a new role for itself. The slogan "out of area or out of business" sums up much of the ongoing intra-NATO debate over the organization's future.

With NATO's fate hanging in the balance, its members have visibly drifted apart. Unable to agree on either the question of membership expansion or conflict resolution in Eastern Europe, NATO members have effectively begun to reconsider the extent to which the alliance should represent their national interests. Although committed to NATO as an organization, alliance members have not entrusted NATO with the necessary authority to take a decisive approach to conflict management beyond the geographical confines of the alliance.

Were NATO to disintegrate outright or continue to linger, as it seems to be doing at present, further renationalization of security can be expected. This could manifest itself most clearly in the adoption of different national approaches to Central and Eastern Europe. Given its geopolitical position and historical connections to the region, Germany might feel compelled to pursue a much more active foreign policy than it currently does, if only to avert the spillover of instability to the east. By contrast, France and especially the U.K. are likely to define their European interests much closer to home, becoming increasingly aloof from events in Europe's other half.

The single most important disincentive to outright or incremental renationalization of security is the professed goal of European union. Since union assumes a common foreign and defense policy, national approaches to issues of European security will have no place. However, this holds true only insofar as European union remains a desirable political goal.

A *third* security option could be the creation of a European concert.[7] Like its ninteenth-century predecessor, this concert would aim to maintain peace through cooperation among Europe's major powers. Since such a system would involve France, Germany and the U.K., as well as Russia, it would be desirable to include the United States to offset Russian might. Such a grouping would be small enough to reach consensus and powerful enough to quell most if not all disturbances to the peace. Effective conflict management could be envisaged and the chances of new conflicts breaking out could be reduced.

The concert system is appealing because to function it requires the commitment of only a small number of countries. In light of Europe's present condition, however, its strength is also its greatest weakness. Instability within the Russian Federation, for example, makes Russia a security problem, not part of the solution. A concert system is unlikely to function when one of its members harbors profound instability on its own territory.

As regards the other members of this potential concert, none of them have shown the kind of leadership required to act decisively. The ability to act quickly offered by a concert system is not synonymous with a willingness to act. As recent conflicts in Europe have shown, agreement between major powers has been easier to obtain on questions of what *not* to do than on those of what to do. Hence, concerts only offer opportunities to those who want to act. That aside, it needs to be asked if the concert option would be acceptable to the rest of Europe. For many Central and Eastern European countries, the notion of management by great powers may not be an attractive solution to security issues. After years of domination, smaller states in the region expect to be involved in a new security system. This is especially the case for states such as Georgia, Ukraine, and the three Baltic republics, for whom relations with Russia are still conflictual. Further, the evolution of Russian foreign policy since the December parliamentary elections suggests its formulation is now much more closely tied to the constraints of forging a domestic consensus on national interests. Russian and Western approaches to security issues can therefore not be expected to be easily reconcilable. A concert would have to be able to expect at least a modicum of a shared vision of what it should accomplish. It may not be possible to obtain it.

A *fourth* path toward European security is offered through collective arrangements. Although much maligned as a security concept far too idealistic to be taken seriously, the appropriateness of a collective security system for Europe is once again being debated.[8] Much of its poor reputation stems from the failure of the League of Nations to organize collective security successfully after World War I. From that experience a lesson presumably emerged: as long as states exist, they are compelled to put the national interest before collective needs. Indeed, as long as the interests of states are at variance with those of the collective, states cannot be expected to act against their national interests, especially when primary security issues are at stake.

The key to making collective security acceptable to states is to make it relevant to their national interests. In other words, the task is to achieve a high degree of convergence between the requirements of the security environment and the national interests of states in it. In a European context, the task is to make states' leaders and opinion makers understand that their nation's interests will be served by creating a security order appropriate for the environment of which they themselves are part. Could collective security be the appropriate security model for the Europe of today and tomorrow?

Among the various options, collective security is the only mechanism offering a truly pan-European path to security. It makes security on the continent every state's right and not the privilege of a few. It does not discriminate against nor does it exclude any one state. It does, however, make conflict resolution the responsibility of all. Given the nature of conflict in present-day Europe, the instabilities that make for an insecure environment, and the profound need for an all-European security structure that provides identity and enhances stability domestically and regionally, a collective security system addresses Europe's needs more comprehensively than any other political option. What, then, are the practical steps required to create conditions favorable to collective security?[9]

Europe already exhibits some features of a collective security system. The OSCE process as a whole, especially its development during the early 1990s, is clearly aimed at institutionalizing its core functions of conflict prevention and mediation. Indeed, there has been a veritable flurry of recent activities, including the establishment of bodies and functions all concerned with forging closer and more cooperative links between the OSCE and the United Nations, the OSCE and the Western European Union (WEU), and the OSCE and the Council of Europe; and the creation of the North Atlantic Cooperation Council (NACC) in early 1992 facilitates exchanges between NATO and the countries of Central and Eastern Europe. The most recent addition to this network of organizations and institutions, the Partnership for Peace, provides another layer of cooperation between West and East.[10]

Collective action has been more apparent than real. Western governments have lent their support to collective designs but have not given them enough substance or resources. Of course, there is a great need to enhance communication between OSCE members, to increase transparency at all levels, and to gather information on developments and issues relevant to security. That said, this kind of activity pales before the need for collective action in situations in which it has not so far been forthcoming. The West, it seems, has acted collectively when real choices about national interests could be avoided. Professed commitment to collective security ought, however, to be judged not on the basis of intention but according to the degree of genuine implementation.

CONCLUSION

The picture that emerges does not suggest an easy or short path to building security across Europe, without which postauthoritarian transitions in the East will be slower and more conflictual. The continent is in the midst of historic changes. Relationships between countries are unsettled, as are domestic relations between rival political groups. There is the continuing danger of states breaking apart and ethnic tensions escalating into open conflict.

Collective security offers the only means of encompassing the whole of Europe and integrating its still disparate parts. Collective incrementalism as currently practiced is unlikely to lead to collective security proper. It raises expectations for a security order that states are not yet willing to adopt. Without a clear recognition that peace in Europe is in the national interest of each and every state, skepticism concerning the notion of a collective security order will be proven right and the concept will remain a desirable but unachievable objective.

NOTES

1. See K. S. Shedai, "Ethnic Self-Determination and the Break-up of States," *Adelphi Papers* no. 283 (December 1993); "International Security Affects the

Soviet Collapse," *Survival* (Spring 1992); "Ethnic Conflict and International Security," *Survival* (Spring 1993).

2. *Atlantic News*, Brussels; see especially issues no. 2578, December 8, 1993, and no. 2583, December 30, 1993.

3. "West's Resolve Disappears into Uncertainty," *Financial Times*, January 24, 1994; "Least Bad Option," *Financial Times*, January 26, 1994; "Who Can Make Peace in Bosnia," *The New York Times*, January 28, 1994.

4. For a country-by-country discussion of the sources of stability and instability, see R. Cowen-Karp, *Central and Eastern Europe—The Challenge of Transition*, SIPRI (Oxford: Oxford University Press, 1993).

5. "Roll Over Reformers," *Financial Times,* January 22/23, 1994; "Russia's New Government," *Financial Times,* January 21, 1994; "Financial Minister Shuns Yeltin Plea and Quits Cabinet," *Financial Times,* January 27, 1994; "Reformers Urge Yeltsin to Resist Policy Switch," *Financial Times,* January 28, 1994.

6. "Russian MPs Want End to Serb Sanctions," *Financial Times*, January 22/23, 1994; "Nationalist Vote Toughens Russian Foreign Policy," *The New York Times*, January 25, 1994.

7. C. Kupcan and C. Kupcan, "Concerts, Collective Security and the Future of Europe," *International Security* 4, no.1 (Summer 1991): 114–161.

8. See Kupcan and Kupcan, "Concerts, Collective Security and the Future of Europe," pp.114–161; A. Bennet and J. Lepgold, "Reinventing Collective Security after the Cold War and the Gulf Conflict," *Political Science Quarterly* 108, no.2 (1993): 213–237; J. Joffe, "Collective Security and the Future of Europe," *Survival* (Spring 1992): 36–50.

9. Some of these steps were addressed in Daniel N. Nelson, "Security in a Post-Hegemonic World," *Bulletin of Peace Proposals* 22, no. 3 (September 1991).

10. A. D. Rotfeld, "The CSCE: Towards a Security Organization," *SIPRI Yearbook 1993: World Armaments and Disarmament* (Oxford: Oxford University Press, 1993), and Appendix SA, 171–218.

Chapter 8

Containing Ethnic Conflict

CHARLES WILLIAM MAYNES

Although the world may worry about a post–Cold War America turning inward, the rhetoric of the last presidential campaign followed by the December 1992 U.S. decision to intervene in Somalia suggested that America was poised for a new burst of foreign policy activism. As a candidate, Bill Clinton, in an April 1, 1992, speech before the Foreign Policy Association, called for America "to lead a global alliance for democracy as united and steadfast as the global alliance that defeated communism." The loser in the last election, George Bush, called in his campaign for a new world order

in which nations settle disputes through cooperation, not confrontation; where the strong protect the weak; where people are governed by the rule of law and not the tyranny of despots; where people are free to choose their own leaders and form of government; and where they can travel and enjoy the fruits of their own labor free from oppression.

Both candidates saw the Gulf War as a harbinger of the post–Cold War world and both supported the intervention in Somalia as another example of post–Cold War internationalism. For Bush, the Gulf War was the "first example of the emerging new world order." In the April 1 speech, Clinton contended that "the role of the United Nations during the Gulf War was a vivid illustration of what is possible in a new era." By mid-January 1993, as the change in power drew near, as the bloody struggle among Croats, Muslims, and Serbs in the former Yugoslavia enveloped all of Bosnia-Herzegovinia, Bill Clinton edged toward intervention. Meanwhile, many pundits and commentators were going further. They were calling for a new approach to international relations, one that would urge humanitarian intervention through collective military action in dealing with ethnic disputes, that would bestow a much larger role on the United Nations (UN), and that would sanction the use of force, if necessary, to defend or impose international norms of legality or political order.

A critical test for the Clinton administration, then, has been how it has dealt with the pressure for a new approach to crises that resemble those in Bosnia-Herzegovina or Somalia. There have been several key questions that required answers from the new president: To what degree can collective security work in dealing with ethnic disputes? Are there other tools available? Is the American approach to ethnic disputes valid for other countries?

The Clinton administration has not, thus far, found the answers to those questions very satisfactory. Collective security probably will not work in most cases. The other tools are politically difficult to use.

Undoubtedly, heightened interest in humanitarian intervention and collective security, particularly in 1992–1993, can be explained in different ways. Endorsement of either or both provides the country's foreign policy elite with a new rationale for its continued relevance in high policy circles now that the Cold War has ended. It also protects political figures from the damaging label of "isolationist." Finally, so long as UN members continue to follow the U.S. lead, no conflict will arise, at least temporarily, between those who support traditional American unilateralism and those who press for new forms of American multilateralism: the United States calls the tune while the rest of the world dances.

The difficulty for the Clinton administration has been and will continue to be that the number of places needing some form of collective security or forcible intervention is growing. Since the Gulf War, all the trends have been in the wrong direction. Rather than the strong protecting the weak, the news has been of cowards firing mortar shells into hospitals and markets in Sarajevo. Instead of people freely enjoying the fruits of their own labor and the rule of law, intolerance and ethnic hatred seem to be spreading across the face of Europe. Not only are the recently liberated peoples of Central and Eastern Europe using their new freedom to act on old hatreds, but ugly racial prejudices are disrupting the most politically stable states of Europe. In 1993, right-wing thugs firebombed innocent foreigners in Germany and a former French prime minister publicly sympathized with compatriots who object to the presence and smell of France's Arab immigrant population.

Indeed, animosity among ethnic groups is beginning to rival the spread of nuclear weapons as the most serious threat to peace that the world faces. No doubt the stakes are high. The conflict between Armenia and Azerbaijan may have had little immediate impact on relations among the great powers, but much larger consequences could flow from the tensions rising between the Russian Federation and the Baltic states. If Russia were to move militarily to protect its conationals in Estonia or Latvia, where they are now being mistreated, a cold peace would develop between Moscow and its Western partners. Many of the hopes for a new, more cooperative world would dim.

Larger issues are also involved in the ethnic tension developing in the Serbian province of Kosovo and in newly independent Macedonia, both of which have large Albanian populations. Albania has already announced that it will act in the event of a conflict between the Albanian majority in Kosovo (of more than 90 percent) and Serbia. Greece and Turkey might then be drawn in. The North Atlantic Treaty Organization (NATO) would be shaken. The conflict could spread further.

In Africa the geopolitical stakes may be lower, but the level of human misery is greater. A vicious cycle of tribal rivalries and governmental collapse has made all talk of a new world order or a crusade for democracy seem a cruel hoax to most Africans.

Somalia is not the only country in trouble; its neighbors are not in much better shape. In Sudan the central authorities from the north, who are Muslim, have attempted to impose *sharia*, or Muslim law, on the south, whose Christian and animist populations insist on autonomy. The civil war has been fought with such cruelty that tens of thousands of children have lost their parents and now roam the Sudanese countryside searching for food and shelter. Most will perish.

Mozambique's long and vicious civil war brought the country to the edge of collapse before the rebel Renamo army and President Chissano reached a fragile cease-fire in October 1992. Ethiopia teeters. On the other side of Africa, from Angola to Liberia, the news is of ethnic conflict, mass misery, and dissolving authority. And the list grows.

Afghanistan is a cauldron of ethnic and religious hatred. There is little foreign interest in the future of Afghans, whose fate was a Western preoccupation as long as the Cold War raged. And in Haiti, a corrupt military continues to exclude an elected president while protecting a mostly mulatto elite by terrorizing a helpless majority of poor blacks.

In short, the balance sheet for the new world order does not look very reassuring. The world appears to be at the beginning, not of a new order, but of a new nightmare.

USING THE UN

Since ethnic conflicts are already so well developed and likely only to get worse, many believe the source of the problem is the world's failure to substitute a new world order based on collective security for the outdated Cold War order that rested on East-West hostility fueled by Soviet and American arms. The old antagonism is gone now that Russia threatens primarily itself and Moscow and Washington no longer see one another as enemies. Why not implement the United Nations Charter as its drafters intended and construct a system of global collective security to deal with the new threats?

In response to that call, Secretary-General Boutros Boutros-Ghali in his June 1992 *Agenda for Peace* proposed an ambitious series of steps, including the creation of a small standing UN force. France and Russia have endorsed the creation of such a force, probably in the belief that they will have a larger voice in peacekeeping if it is directed through the UN than if it is organized on an ad hoc basis by Washington. The U.S. government under Bush reserved judgment on the secretary-general's proposal, but in his campaign speeches Clinton suggested the value of a UN rapid deployment force, which "could be used for purposes beyond traditional peacekeeping, such as standing guard at the borders of countries threatened by aggression; preventing more violence against civilian populations; providing humanitarian relief; and combating terrorism." (Despite the multiple tasks, he argued that it would "not be a large standing army but rather a small force that could be called up from units of national armed forces and earmarked and trained in advance.")

The demand for a reinvigorated UN peacekeeping effort is understandable given the many crises that are erupting around the world. But unless care is taken, UN or other peacekeeping forces could be involved in extremely dangerous situations, in which they might be unable to accomplish the goals that reformers have in mind. Most recent commentary fails to recognize, for example, that the UN system, though drawn up in the universal language of collective security, in which the common enemy appears to be aggression from any source, did in effect identify the likely opponents. They were the enemy states, Germany and Japan, covered in Articles 53 and 107 of the Charter. Discussions at the time the Charter was drafted make clear the general concern of member states over a resurgent Germany or Japan. In other words, a system providing a veto to the five victorious powers could work as long as they had a common enemy, and in 1945 they believed they did.

Is it possible to develop a similar consensus that instability per se is the enemy? It seems unlikely. Washington and Moscow probably went as far as possible in their cooperation in the former Yugoslavia, for example, when the Clinton administration endorsed the Russian role in guaranteeing Serb compliance with a NATO/UN ultimatum to remove artillery around Sarajevo. A formal decision to target Serbia militarily would probably have broken the consensus. The Russian government had been under attack from right-wing nationalists—most prominently, Vladimir Zhirinovsky—for abandoning its traditional ally, Serbia. The early 1994 reentry of Russia into Balkan politics, then, gave Yeltsin an important defense against such nationalist criticisms.

Certainly, unless the veto could be set aside, the UN would be incapable of doing anything more than offer good offices in the event of a conflict between Russia and one of its neighbors. But even in more distant parts of the world, it is unrealistic to expect that the five countries with a veto on the Security Council, particularly China and Russia, will always be able to agree. From the beginning, therefore, in order to avoid unreasonable expectations, those in favor of UN reform must be realistic in their claims. It is highly unlikely that the Gulf War will really turn out to be a model for the future.

Another common mistake in discussions of UN reform involves a confusion of peacekeeping with peace observing. In the past, UN troops were called peacekeepers when they were really peace observers. They were deployed only upon the agreement of the parties in conflict. They were lightly armed and were able to defend themselves only against isolated attacks, not against a major assault by a professional army. When one of the parties benefiting from a peacekeeping agreement decided to abrogate its terms, the UN forces were helpless. In 1967, Egypt demanded that the UN troops separating Israel from Egypt be withdrawn. Eventually, the UN had no alternative but to withdraw them. (The secretary-general should have procrastinated in the hope that the Egyptians would come to their senses, or that outside states would bring pressure to bear on Cairo to change its position, but that is another story.)

When the Israelis told the UN troops separating Israel and the Palestine Liberation Organization in southern Lebanon to get out of the way in 1982, again the UN had no alternative but to bend to Israeli wishes and look on as the Israelis invaded Lebanon. Neither in 1967 nor in 1982 was the UN in a military position to resist an army as large as Egypt's or Israel's. The peacekeepers could only stay as long as both wished them to stay.

Sometimes additional confusion develops because there is talk of using a UN peacekeeping force as a trip wire. But except in unusual circumstances UN peacekeeping troops cannot be equated with, say, the U.S. forces in West Berlin during the Cold War, which did serve a trip wire function. In the case of the American troops in Berlin, Moscow knew that if they were attacked, there was a significant probability that military hostilities with the United States would ensue. In the case of UN troops in the Sinai or southern Lebanon, Cairo and Jerusalem knew that if UN troops attempted to bar the way and therefore were attacked, there was a very low probability of a UN military response. The patron of each side could be expected to use the veto.

The United States, in the hubris of the Reagan administration, forgot the fundamental nature of peacekeeping. It deployed U.S. marines in Lebanon without understanding that it was essential for their safety that the United States not take sides in the Lebanese civil war. The Reagan administration decided to back the Christians and soon found its troops under attack by the Muslims and finally driven from Lebanon after the disastrous bombing of the marine barracks in Beirut.

Much of the confusion about peacekeeping has developed because of the unusual circumstances in which UN peacekeepers have found themselves in both Lebanon and Bosnia-Herzegovina. In both operations the UN deployments have enjoyed the formal approval of the concerned governments. But for the first time since the Congo operation in the early 1960s—a crisis that nearly destroyed the UN—the world body has found its troops regularly attacked by forces that are not under the control of central governments. Iran, Israel, or Syria may influence the various militias in Lebanon, but no outside force can control them completely. And certainly the government of Lebanon cannot. In such circumstances, whether UN troops can continue to perform their traditional functions depends on the extent of the challenge. If isolated attacks grow to where a large segment of the local population opposes the UN presence, its options are complete withdrawal or the invasion of the country with a force sufficient to compel compliance with UN mandates. The latter course of action is unacceptable to the international community because of the bloodshed and expense involved.

In Bosnia the situation is even more complicated. If Serbia is in adequate control of those forces in Bosnia that have violated various UN-negotiated cease-fires, then the appropriate response is to persuade Serbia to end the defiance of UN mandates either by reaching an understanding with Belgrade or, if necessary, by compelling Belgrade through military force. But if the militias are assisted rather than controlled by Serbia, then the UN's options depend on the extent of the local challenge to the UN forces. If that challenge moves beyond isolated attacks to the point of war against UN forces, then the UN must either withdraw from Bosnia-Herzegovina or prepare for the occupation of the country by a force large enough to suppress presumably fierce Serbian resistance. Because that task could involve hundreds of thousands of troops, the great powers have been understandably reluctant to act. Despite the withdrawal of most Serb artilleries from around Sarajevo in February 1994, when NATO air attacks were threatened, suggestions that air power alone could settle the issue seem specious. Serbs greatly outnumber the Muslims in the former Yugoslavia and the Serbs are better armed. Air attacks on the Serbs are likely to lead to even greater Serbian pressure on the Muslims, who have received outside supplies only at the sufferance of the Serbs. The West would then be faced with the need to come to the rescue of the Muslims with military operations on the ground.

The best course for the international community, therefore, is a final effort to reach an agreement by negotiation. If that fails, then the United Nations should respect the demand of the authorities in Sarajevo that they be given the tools to defend themselves. With outside help and even air support, they still would be unlikely to win the war but they might limit the size of a new greater Serbia enough to carve out a place for the Muslim minority to retain their own state. No one should doubt, however, that such a solution would bring even more killing and ethnic cleansing.

It is important to understand the root of the problem in Bosnia-Herzegovina or Somalia. It is not ineptitude on the part of the UN or the European Community or the United States, though all three have made serious mistakes in those crises. The fundamental issue was underscored in a 1992 Brookings Institution study of cooperative security, which stated that

as the bloodshed in Yugoslavia and Somalia reveals, the international community does not have the security mechanism that would be required to control serious civil violence. The available apparatus of diplomatic mediation backed by the imposition of economic sanctions or even by threatened military intervention requires a corresponding political structure to have any constructive effect.

But to create such a structure would require what might be called the World War II solution: the total defeat of the sanctioned country, the imposition of a new political order there, and a lengthy occupation until the international community was sure that new and more acceptable institutions had taken root. A World War II solution is what the world seemed to be edging toward in Somalia because the cost to the international community appeared to be manageable. But even there the great powers were unwilling to make the commitment required: after street battles in Mogadishu that left dozens of U.S. troops dead or wounded, the United States backed away from action to disarm the country and withdrew forces by March 1994. Several of the other governments participating in the occupation withdrew their troops simultaneously with the departure of U.S. troops, and the UN is hesitant to confront the need to establish some form of medium-term trusteeship over Somalia until normal life can be restored.

But suppose that the international community had taken all those steps in Somalia. The problems of all the other UN members that are suffering from civil unrest would remain. Already African governments are suggesting UN or U.S. intervention in other ethnic conflicts on their continent. Clearly the UN cannot intervene in every ethnic conflict around the globe. The world must find other ways to address the problems of tribalism and group conflict before the hatred and mistrust are such that only outside military intervention is likely to succeed, yet is unavailable.

DIVIDED SOCIETIES

In searching for those other tools, the world must recognize that, in regions like the former Yugoslavia or parts of the former Soviet Union, it is facing the kind of crisis for which it has never had a satisfactory answer. In this century, when two or more populations have been reluctant to live with one another in a single state, the options open to the international community have turned out to be either unconscionable or unpalatable: ethnic cleansing, repression, partition, or power sharing. Of the four, ethnic cleansing ironically appears the most politically effective, albeit the most morally reprehensible. Despite the human costs, Poland and the Czech Republic are more stable today because they were permitted to eject their German minorities. So are Greece and Turkey after they carried out massive exchanges of populations in the 1920s. But at the personal and community level such exchanges are exceedingly cruel and they were only tolerated because the wars they followed had set new standards of cruelty. The world today will rightly be much less tolerant of a state demanding the right to ethnic purity.

Repression has been another answer to ethnic conflict. It was the communist answer throughout Eastern Europe and in the Soviet Union itself. It is the Syrian answer in Lebanon today. It is an answer that provides a temporary solution today but prepares the way for a political explosion tomorrow. Those repressed only await the day when they can rise up. The world tolerates Syrian repression in Lebanon today only because it seems somewhat more benign than the ethnic and religious anarchy that roiled Lebanese politics from the mid-1970s on. It is a miserable solution to an intractable problem.

Partition along with some form of ethnic cleansing was the world's solution in Palestine and South Asia. The difficulty with partition is that the line cannot be drawn with any exactitude. Significant minorities will be left behind. New ones will be exposed or develop. Partition has been impossible in Bosnia-Herzegovina because the Croats, Muslims, and Serbs have been mixed.

Power sharing is the most humane approach to the problem of ethnic conflict, but that is not to deny its unusual political difficulty. As John Stuart Mill pronounced in *Representative Government*, democracy is "next to impossible" in a country with a multiethnic population. The authorities in ethnically divided Bosnia-Herzegovina at first sought a unified state. The Serbs feared they would be permanently outvoted. Now, under the pressure of a civil war, all sides are discussing power sharing with UN mediator Cyprus Vance and European Community representative David Owen. Power sharing in Zimbabwe took place only after years of civil war. It fell apart in Lebanon because demographic changes called into question the legitimacy of the power-sharing formula.

For power sharing to work in some of the ethnic conflicts that now trouble world peace, however, much more needs to be known about how different societies have attempted to resolve their ethnic conflicts. A 1972 study of conflict resolution in divided states by political scientist Eric Nordlinger did identify several key principles: agreed outcomes, proportionality, mutual vetoes, and "purposive depoliticization." Thus, conflicts are often reduced when party leaders make pre- or postelection deals (agreed outcomes) that accord the defeated parties a place at the table. Societies as different as Austria and Malaysia have reduced bitter ethnic or religious conflicts through a political process of negotiated outcomes. Regardless of election results, the numerically weaker party knew it would still have a voice in national politics.

Many ethnically or politically divided states have tamped down conflict by a proportional division of key offices. Examples of such states include Belgium and pre-1975 Lebanon. Each ethnic group was assured a certain number of key positions.

Frightened minorities may also be reassured by a system of mutual vetoes. Both Austria and Belgium have sought civil peace through such a system. No decision can be made without all key parties agreeing. "Purposive depoliticization" involves an agreement among all parties that certain subjects are outside politics—for example, religion. States that have followed that path include Belgium, Lebanon, and the Netherlands.

The final principle Nordlinger identifies is perhaps the most difficult of all and is rarely practiced. The history of ethnic conflicts suggests that they may be reduced if the stronger group is willing to make the major concessions. In Switzerland, for example, even though the Protestant majority won the civil war in 1847, it made major concessions to the defeated Catholics, who were offered equal representation even though some of their districts were smaller. The gesture was so successful that within a year the defeated cantons had declared that they "would offer their services to the Bund and fight in its army at the slightest sign of a threat to Switzerland from the outside."

Perhaps one reason the United States held together as a democracy after the Civil War is that Abraham Lincoln asked for "malice toward none" and "charity for all." The South, though crushed, regained from the victorious North equal representation in Congress. Indeed, through the seniority system in Congress, the South acquired disproportionate power in the federal government. More recently, white Americans, though a majority, under the pressure of the civil rights movement, accepted limitations on majority rights in the form of affirmative action and other racially directed policies. While those limitations have been extremely controversial, they have not been rejected because the national goal is civic peace. Now, through oddly shaped, gerrymandered districts, the American political system, in the interests of racial harmony, is going so far as to effectively guarantee more seats in Congress for African Americans and Hispanic Americans.

Ironically, studies of ethnic conflict suggest that some of the remedies that Americans assume can address the problem are, in fact, not effective.[1] For example, Americans tend to focus on individual rights rather than on group rights. That is a feature of what might be called Anglo-American democracy. But many European democracies practice what is known as "consociational democracy," which offers greater accommodation to group rights and more protection to those who feel vulnerable in a "winner take all" system of democracy. European practice seems much more appropriate for the ethnically or religiously driven conflicts that are now troubling the world.

Americans are big believers in federalism. But specialists in ethnic conflict are wary of federal solutions because they tend to promote secession or partition and even greater intolerance toward the minority groups that are left behind.

Finally, a recent feature of American diplomacy in several administrations has been a strong belief in the need to negotiate from strength. That position, more appropriate for a Cold War struggle, is then applied to other conflicts where it is asserted that no one should win at the negotiation table what has not already been won on the battlefield or through the ballot box. But deeply rooted ethnic, religious, or ideological struggles are not resolved that way. Not understanding that concept, Americans are puzzled when an election in Angola does not end the conflict or when the victorious party in Nicaragua deems it necessary to reach out to the defeated Sandinistas.

The international community needs to know more about what works and what does not in the handling of ethnic or religious conflict. The UN Security Council should commission a study of successful attempts to resolve such conflicts and hold a meeting at the foreign minister level to discuss the results. Leaders in the international community need to understand past successes better so that they may deal more effectively with the crises of today.

PROVISIONS FOR PEACE

Armed with better knowledge, what additional steps might the world community take? First, the international community needs to dramatically improve the UN's ability to practice preventive diplomacy so ethnic or religious tensions can be addressed before they erupt into violence. Member states have long denied the secretary-general the eyes and ears that would enhance his organization's ability to intervene early and effectively in crises that threaten international peace and security. He has no ambassadors or embassies. He has been discouraged from deploying fact finders to investigate crises. He has not been permitted to take advantage of new breakthroughs in satellite intelligence, although at one point INTELSAT did offer to reserve three channels on its satellites for the UN.

To provide the UN the eyes and ears needed, the intelligence agencies of the great powers, searching for a new mission with the end of the Cold War, could provide weekly briefings to the secretary-general or senior UN officials. (There is much criticism of the U.N. for not alerting the world in time to the disaster in Somalia. But where were the intelligence agencies of the major powers?) The secretary-general could be authorized to buy time regularly on the French satellite surveillance service (SPOT) that is now available commercially. Moreover, since 1986 the French have proposed a

U.N. satellite for gathering information and monitoring developments around the globe. That would be a more useful but a more expensive option.

There are, of course, provisions in the Charter that, if used, would enhance the world's ability to practice preventive diplomacy. Article 99 permits the secretary-general to bring to the Council's attention any situation he deems a threat to peace. But he must know enough about the situation to be sure of his ground. He could draw on Article 99 to dispatch fact-finding missions on his own authority, as Dag Hammarskjöld did—to America's dismay—when he visited China in January 1955; but even if it should be used more often, Article 99 must be used sparingly. Its regular use without the support of the Security Council could deprive the secretary-general of his authority. Rather, the great powers should exploit Article 34 of the Charter, which states that the Security Council "may investigate any dispute or any situation which might lead to international friction or give rise to a dispute." That provision should be used to create anticipatory fact-finding and mediation efforts in crisis spots from the Baltic states to the Horn of Africa.

Second, the international community must begin to redefine the obligations of nation-states so that minority rights receive greater protection. Moral approval must go to the civil state, which seeks to provide a decent life for all of its citizens, rather than to the ethnic state, which provides a home for a dominant nationality. Prince Bernhard von Bülow, the former German chancellor, wrote in 1914 that "in the struggle between nationalities one nation is the hammer, the other the anvil, one is the victor and one is the vanquished." That was the logic employed by Adolf Hitler in asserting the rights of German nationalism over all others. Today's German state is light-years away from the kind of Germany envisaged by either of those leaders, but it still continues a troubling tradition that makes it extremely difficult for non-Germans who have lived for decades in Germany to receive German citizenship. The law effectively brands all foreigners in Germany as not belonging there and so encourages ethnic violence. Japan is another state that has similarly tough citizenship laws. Moral approval for such an approach to citizenship must be withdrawn. And the American approach to ethnic conflict is, on the whole, wrongheaded and needs to be changed, as disscussed above.

In promoting the civil state, the UN could look to the League of Nations in the treatment of minorities. The peace treaties of 1919 required states such as Czechoslovakia, Greece, Poland, and Romania to assure full protection to all inhabitants without distinctions of birth and nationality, language, race, or religion. Meanwhile, the League worked out a procedure for the settlement of minority disputes. True, those treaties were flawed. They were too vague. The most powerful states, such as Germany, did not accept comparable obligations toward their minorities. There were no sanctions for those who ignored their provisions. But the treaties represented the first attempt in history to provide international legal protection to minority populations.

Unfortunately, instead of building on those treaties after World War II, UN members gave far less attention to the issue of minority rights. The Soviet Union, with its many minorities, did not want a strong UN interest in their fate. And the United States had its own concerns because of its large African-American minority, many of whom were then denied the right to vote. The UN human rights machinery remained more concerned with individual rights than with minority rights.

That attitude is changing. At the 1992 General Assembly, UN members adopted a resolution on minority rights that stated that persons belonging to such minorities have the right to enjoy their own culture, to profess and practice their own religion, and to use their own language. However, much more needs to be done. UN members should take advantage of the proposed June 1993 meeting in Vienna of the World Conference on Human Rights to begin to develop the concept of the civil state over the ethnic state. An effort should be made to codify strong obligations that all member states would accept with respect to minorities.

Today, the Third World fears that the developed countries will use human rights to resurrect neocolonialism. The fears are so great that the Vienna meeting is in danger. To combat those fears, the major states, including the United States, should make it clear that all states, including the great states, will accept the same responsibilities with respect to minorities. At the Vienna meeting, the United States should press for the creation of working groups that could publicly monitor the record of all states in that sensitive area. The UN Security Council should also develop sanctions to be applied against states that violate their international obligations—denial of access to international capital markets and international financial institutions or suspension of their membership in international institutions.

Realistically, world opinion alone cannot prevent a large state from mistreating its minorities if it is determined to do so. But criticism, ostracism, and sanctions can affect decision making. And most states are not in a position to defy the international community totally. As horrible as the events in the former Yugoslavia have been, it is instructive that in the face of vigorous international criticism, which was late to develop, the Serbs opened several concentration camps to inspections by the UN and the Red

Cross and began releasing many of the prisoners. Part of the tragedy of the former Yugoslavia rests in the fact that, because the UN has no independent intelligence capability and the great powers do not share their intelligence with it, the appalling conditions in the camps were not news until so many had perished.

Third, in order to reduce Third World fears of great power intervention in their internal affairs, part of any international effort to ensure minority rights must be a strengthening of regional organizations. Many developing countries are reluctant to see the Security Council, dominated by five permanent members, of which four are former colonial powers, as the chief enforcement instrument of intervention to maintain international peace and security and to protect minority rights. Indeed, although they deserve membership, making Germany and Japan permanent members of the Security Council will only compound the problem.

There is, in fact, a growing body of evidence to suggest that regional organizations can play a constructive role in sorting out seemingly intractable disputes. The Contadora Group of Latin American states was able to influence the outcome of the civil wars in Central America in a constructive direction, and West African states were able to intervene in Liberia during a cruel civil war, even if difficulties remain. The Association of Southeast Asian Nations (ASEAN) played a substantial role in facilitating the UN peace process that led to the signing of the settlement plan for Cambodia.

It will be objected that the world cannot depend on regional organizations to show the necessary courage. Last July, for example, the ASEAN countries remained silent on human rights abuses in Burma while the United States was urging the region to take a stronger position. The Organization for African Unity remained silent about Ugandan dictator Idi Amin until he had finally lost power. The Arab League has examined Israel's human rights record with a microscope while turning a blind eye toward much worse abuses in the Arab world.

The way to change that reality is to again exploit the UN Charter. It provides that regional organizations cannot undertake enforcement action without the authorization of the Security Council. That provision of the Charter could be used to develop over time a greater degree of accountability on the part of regional organizations. To date, the Security Council has not made relationships with regional groups a priority.

The Security Council's credibility would be enhanced if its composition were changed. But a Charter amendment to grant permanent seats to countries like Germany and Japan is likely to take time. Meanwhile, the council has the right to create suborgans. For the purposes of peacekeeping missions, the council should create a subcommission, on which Germany and Japan would be regular members, for the direction and financing of peacekeeping operations. In addition, before the UN authorized a fact-finding or mediation or peacekeeping operation in a particular region of the world, key states from the region should become members of the subcommittee.

Finally, the world community should never rule out the use of force in principle. Often, when debating the use of force, the UN seems paralyzed by the prospect of a double standard: how can it intervene in one country when it refuses to do so in another? But the impossibility of intervening everywhere should not bar the UN from acting anywhere. The international community must accept the inevitability of what might be called *opportunistic idealism*. Thus, one would not have wanted to prevent the dispatch of troops to Somalia simply because the international community was unwilling or unable to take similar actions in other parts of the world. But it is important to understand that the world community will rarely use force to control ethnic and religious conflicts. The international community has neither the will nor the capacity to intervene militarily in such situations. It needs other tools.

The development of such tools need not stand in the way of moving toward the bolder visions outlined by Bush and Clinton in the 1992 presidential campaign. The UN could, for example, create a standing force composed of volunteers who would be willing to undertake dangerous operations under the UN flag. To prepare for the occasional emergency in which a much larger force might be needed, UN members, including the United States, could earmark national forces for peacekeeping tasks. Those forces could be trained to respond quickly, within a few days, to a UN request with which the host government was in agreement. Earmarked forces might train together, and governments providing troops could be invited to join a Security Council subcommittee that would oversee the training and preparation of the forces. But all should understand that the permanent UN force will be far too small to intervene in the many ethnic conflicts from which the world now suffers, and member states may be reluctant to offer earmarked troops for an enforcement action.

Some, especially those sensitive to current U.S. financial difficulties, might ask why the world should organize a UN force that would be used infrequently and would be so clearly unequal to the larger task. The answer lies in a belief that a UN effort to enhance minority rights legally and UN tools diplomatically and militarily would represent a global commitment to act that is now missing even on those occasions where multinational military involvement is both possible and likely to be effective. Help in Somalia, for example, might have been provided much earlier if UN members had already accepted the legal and financial commitments involved in the creation of new legal instruments, new institutional structures, and new military forces. Instead of procrastinating and then insisting that the UN effort be voluntary in order to save money—the initial U.S. position—major powers might have been more inclined to use instruments already in place and paid for.

In the end, of course, the primary need is not for more conflict, even under a UN flag. The need is for more diplomacy—early, persistent, and effective. Even if the world gains that kind of diplomacy, no one can guarantee that violence will never erupt again as it has in Bosnia or Somalia. But the number of such conflicts can be reduced, the lives of millions improved, and UN members brought closer to their Charter obligations. It would not be a new world order, but it would also not be an ignoble goal for an activist administration.

NOTES

This Chapter is reprinted with permission from *Foreign Policy* (Spring 1993). Copyright 1993 by the Carnegie Endowment for International Peace.

1. See Arend Lijphart, *Democracy in Plural Societies* (New Haven, Conn.: Yale University Press, 1977) and Eric A. Nordlinger, *Conflict Regulation in Divided Societies* (Cambridge, Mass.: Harvard Center for International Affairs, 1972).

Chapter 9

Leadership in a Transitional World: The Challenge of Keeping the Peace

PAUL DAVID MILLER

A CHANGING WORLD

The world we knew seems indeed to have disappeared in the blink of an eye. Yet no real order has emerged to take its place. We find ourselves in a transitional period, in which a classical balance of power no longer functions. Our expectations about the workings of international politics, shaped in a now bygone era, provide few guidelines for shaping the future. National governments and international organizations are hard-pressed to adapt to the dynamic environment. By failing to adapt, governments and institutions could well be judged irrelevant to the new realities.

Individuals and groups thus will play a more prominent role in the emerging transnational setting. The global information revolution permits the instantaneous, uncensored broadcast of world events to anyone with a radio or a television. This revolution is a two-edged sword; on the one hand, it equips the average citizen with the knowledge and confidence to be a productive participant in policy debates, but on the other, it can propel and escalate events in one part of the world into a transnational problem. More important, the global information network holds the potential for dramatically affecting national agendas with its ability to communicate human suffering in compelling, graphic images. We must be willing to evaluate the merits and appropriateness of existing security arrangements solely upon the basis of their ability to deal with such new realities. As we do so, three elements of national and alliance security policy will continue to be viewed as determinative.

First, the fundamental interests of the United States, and its objectives in foreign and defense policy, will remain largely unchanged despite radical changes in the world.[1] Four principles will continue to form the foundations of American strategic policy:

- *Core Security*: The ability to protect the United States through ensuring the ability to deter and defend across the full spectrum of conflict.

- *Crisis Response*: The ability to deploy rapidly the force packages required to deter a conflict or, if necessary, to protect U.S. national interests.

- *Regional Interaction*: The ability to remain engaged globally through bilateral and alliance relationships, as well as ad hoc security coalitions.

- *Reconstitution*: The ability to expand military capability in order to forestall a future military competition when determined by warning indicators.

Second, the North Atlantic Treaty Organization (NATO) must evolve further. There is presently both an opportunity and a need for NATO to serve as an organizing hub for responses to regional or global threats. The alliance provides an appropriate forum for dialogue and cooperation among member states. The alliance's North Atlantic Cooperation Council (NACC) fosters collaboration and mutual understanding among the entire European community. Most specifically, NATO and its individual member states possess capabilities that can contribute to a range of global stabilization, mediation, and crisis resolution activities. Of primary importance is NATO's experience in commanding, and operating within, a multiservice, multinational (or, in the military lexicon, a joint and combined) environment. Specifically, the capabilities NATO or its members can contribute include the following:

- The existing command, control, communication, computer, and intelligence (C^4I) infrastructure, uniquely able to facilitate multinational command and control.

- A technical base and training programs to assist and prepare multinational coalitions.

- NATO procedures, concept plans, and rules of engagement (ROE) for the coordination of multinational operations, which can be quickly adapted to the requirements of collective security coalitions.

- Common and national logistical capabilities, which can provide needed support services to diverse, multinational coalitions.

- Highly trained and proficient command cells and military units, which can serve as observers, mediators, peacekeeping forces, and command elements for various multinational coalitions.

Even when not directly involved in a security coalition, NATO can serve as a model for organizing, training, and commanding multinational forces engaged in collective defense.

Third, the United States—with its global reach and global interests—will continue to be looked to for leadership within both the NATO alliance and the global community. The United States is more than a preeminent economic and military power. American leadership has a strong moral component, founded upon our traditional belief in human rights, the rule of law, and a desire to promote a prosperous and just society.

These three elements comprise a core of continuity. Other security issues have arisen, however, which require us to undertake a basic reassessment. Prominent among these issues is peacekeeping. Conflicts today are increasingly multifactional, with little if any control exercised by a leadership cell. Thus, one issue that must be soon faced is the relevancy of classical peacekeeping to the emerging risks to security—a consideration already prompting bottom-up reviews in Washington, in other world capitals, and within the alliance. These reviews go beyond roles and missions; they start with reassessing the basic security paradigm. The impact of such a review on our stabilization, mediation, and conflict resolution efforts is already becoming clear: peacekeeping operations, as conceived and developed in the Cold War, have been overwhelmed by an increasingly turbulent, transnational world. The command and control mechanisms that evolved for managing peacekeeping operations are inadequate for the crises facing the world community today.

A PROPOSED BLUEPRINT FOR THE FUTURE

> The Wall is gone! But how long will it take to overcome the wall in our minds?
> Graffito on a remaining segment of the Berlin Wall

The end of the Cold War offers both the opportunity and the requirement for developing innovative approaches to the resolution of global crises. Three ideas in particular have merit for facilitating peace-enabling missions in our dynamic and troubled world. These are adaptive capabilities packages, unified command and control network (out of theater), and multifunctional action groups.

These three concepts move planning for the conflicts of the future beyond the discarded paradigm of the Cold War. When endorsed by appropriate civilian decision makers, they can together serve as a blueprint for effective and efficient stabilization, mediation, and conflict resolution efforts.

While much is demanded from the United States, the American people cannot be expected to bear the burden of every crisis in every part of the world. The American challenge, as a former Defense Department official has observed, is to

face those myriad instabilities with balance, creativity, and clear-headedness, mediating where America can play a constructive role, containing or easing threats where appropriate, and prudently ignoring those that can do them no harm. In this pursuit, U.S. political and economic diplomacy must be preeminent, with American military power playing a supporting but nonetheless important role. In concert with other states, the United States can provide security guarantees as a basis for settlement that would otherwise be impossible. It can help selected friendly governments ameliorate some sources of instability by providing humanitarian, infrastructure, and military assistance. And, when instability generates a sufficiently serious threat to American interests, U.S. military power can be used to contain it.[2]

An Adaptive Capabilities Package

In the NATO alliance, the United States, Russia, and elsewhere, military planners are adapting to a new security environment. Hostilities today are more diverse, the contending forces less organized and more factional, and the permanent settlement of conflicts more elusive. The task of reengineering forces for the roles and missions demanded in this changed security environment requires new thinking and new approaches.

There are two possible structuring concepts for military forces assigned to the missions of mediation, stabilization, and crisis resolution. One may either create specialized units for peacekeeping, peace-enforcing, and peace-building missions, or adapt existing forces to meet the requirements. Both approaches have merit; nations must select the option that best suits their needs and requirements.

The approach now being implemented by the Russian military, for example, is illustrative of the first option; the Russian press announced in 1993 the formation of a special peacekeeping force. Specialization of units is a Russian military tradition. The requirement for a Russian peacekeeping force results primarily from the unfortunate reality that ethnic unrest and secessionist warfare is presently occurring in some of the republics of the former Soviet Union (and, indeed, in some areas within the Russian Federation). The Russian peacekeepers will be used—when it is deemed appropriate—to separate the warring factions, monitor crisis areas, and quell small clashes in the absence of any agreement.

The American tradition, however, is different; we adapt our forces for the task at hand. Stated succinctly, the U.S. military is a multidimensional organization composed of basic, intermediate, advanced, and ready-deployable forces. As the units progress through the blocks, they enhance both their service-specific and joint capabilities. Within the U.S. armed forces, we can identify and emphasize the capabilities required by an emerging mission, and blend them with the complementary capabilities of other government agencies and nongovernmental organizations. This can be done at the national, regional, and international level—permitting U.S. armed forces to operate effectively in joint, multiagency, and multinational environments.

As we rethink military roles and missions, and work to reengineer our forces accordingly, the starting point is to identify key elements of military capability—what we refer to as core competencies. Core competencies can serve as an organizing principle guiding the following: the way we identify, select, train, and assemble forces as "packages" of total capability to be deployed forward and applied to specific missions; the way we blend military capabilities with other needed capabilities contributed by civilian government agencies and organizations; and the way we will combine national and alliance capabilities with those of other nations and international organizations, in order to meet the objectives of the international community of responsible nations.

Core competencies need to be properly "packaged" to have real utility. General Colin Powell, chairman of the Joint Chiefs of Staff, and the commanders of the Unified Commands in the U.S. military are currently at work developing Adaptive Joint Force Packages—specific capabilities deployed for a given period, supported by designated backup units that remain in the United States. The concept involves two steps: first, adapting forces to specific regional requirements by drawing needed capabilities from each service; and second, organizing and training those joint forces so that they can be positioned forward when and where required.

With the development of both theater and maritime "reaction forces," the alliance is developing a similar concept. These forces form the vanguard of alliance contributions to crisis resolution operations. In the same way that the United States assembles and deploys a force package from among Army,

Navy, Marine Corps, Air Force, and Special Forces capabilities to meet specific contingency operations, NATO can assemble a regional response package from its multinational immediate reaction, rapid reaction, area, and maritime forces, combined with land and air components of the Allied Command Europe Rapid Reaction Corps (ARRC). This total force package provides a flexible menu of capabilities for NATO's civilian authorities which can be tailored and rapidly deployed in response to any contingency. Adaptive packaging provides a natural mechanism for all alliance members to contribute to the common security objectives of NATO, while permitting member states to contribute according to their military strengths and political prerogatives.

The adaptive force concept also provides an appropriate mechanism for integrating national and alliance capabilities with those of additional contributors—the militaries of other partner states, police forces, relief agencies, election monitors, and the United Nations (UN). Each nation—regardless of size—has capabilities that it can offer toward the overall objective of collective security. If we only speak in terms of battalions, naval task forces, and air wings, we miss the true meaning of responsibility sharing. It does not matter whether a nation volunteers a handful of individuals or a complete battalion from its military; what matters is the willingness and ability to contribute.

A full force package provides the potential range of capabilities and expertise available from the international community—governments, nongovernmental organizations, and regional security alliances. Too often, we overlook the capabilities that exist outside government. As an illustration, the contributions of the International Committee of the Red Cross (ICRC) to global relief efforts are significant and often essential.[3] In Somalia, the ICRC had nine hundred kitchens and fed more than one million people daily. ICRC medical teams performed approximately 250 surgical procedures weekly, and mobile surgical teams treated emergency cases while training local staffs. More than 1,260 metric tons of seed and 18,000 hand tools were distributed to farmers. Similarly, in the former Yugoslavia the ICRC has been delivering parcels consisting of basic food and hygiene products, and providing critical medical supplies to hospitals. And in Mozambique, the Red Cross is providing food assistance, operating therapeutic feeding programs for malnourished children and pregnant women in all drought-affected provinces, rehabilitating wells, and digging latrines in reception centers established for drought-displaced persons.

With such capabilities available from potential international contributors, it is important to develop mechanisms for integrating these capabilities into an effective and efficient team. A particular crisis resolution effort may not (indeed, likely will not) require the use of an entire range of capabilities; the appropriate civilian authorities, with advice from functional specialists, must select the specific capabilities required for a given situation. An adapted capabilities package is one possible configuration. An adaptive multinational force package concept is both flexible and economical.

For such ready-response packages to realize their full promise, the potential contributors to an overall force should be

- Trained and exercised in the same way they would actually be deployed.

- Supported by an appropriate command, control, communication, computer, intelligence, and information (C^4I^2) infrastructure.

- Equipped with the necessary guidance for conducting stabilization, mediation, and crisis resolution operations—what we in the military refer to as joint doctrine.

Training Support and Combined Exercises

Participating personnel need to train and exercise together their contributing capabilities. Regardless of skills or readiness levels, both military and civilian participants need to be familiar with the capabilities of other participants. The real work of forging a team can only begin when participants become less of a mystery to each other. Understanding capabilities is one thing; seeing capabilities employed is quite another. The aircraft carrier is illustrative. Most naval officers are familiar with the routine of a carrier. Others would be amazed at the hectic pace, the noise, the multiplicity of activities, the exhaustive coordination. Being there and seeing the carrier in operation makes all the difference.

In this overall training effort, the United States, the NATO allies, and Russia can contribute the technical base and educational programs needed to train personnel participating in ad hoc coalitions. In addition, including potential coalition partners in both national and alliance exercises—expanded to include mediation and peacekeeping scenarios—can assist in enhancing the readiness and preparedness of their forces.

Standing military units and police forces can easily adapt their operational skills to different operational environments:

Many of the skills which enable a unit to accomplish its primary mission are applicable in peacekeeping. Command and control, reporting, patrolling, first aid, field conditions, field sanitation, and physical fitness are skills which can contribute to success in a peacekeeping operation. Training to enhance these skills should be a part of any pre-deployment training program which would include, as a minimum, the following common military skills: intelligence; observing and reporting; communications; patrolling; navigation; explosive ordnance [disposal]; locating, identifying, and marking mines; and chemical, biological, and radiation defense.[4]

Reserve forces, on the other hand, may require substantial refresher courses. Nordic troops specifically earmarked by their national commanders for UN peacekeeping operations, for instance, are reservists. The Norwegian "total defense" concept is illustrative. There is a normal nine-to-twelve month conscription service, after which the soldier is assigned to a mobilization unit—which receives refresher training limited to a one-week period every three to five years. It can be expected that these forces would require intensive training in basic military skills prior to a UN peacekeeping deployment. In-place training programs would help facilitate the readiness of such reserve forces.

Training is the first step; validating the training through a comprehensive exercise program would follow. To provide a realistic practice field upon which to drill the skills needed for peacekeeping operations, for example, the staffs of both the United States Atlantic Command and NATO's Supreme Allied Commander Atlantic are evaluating options for modifying two scheduled exercises—the Tradewinds exercise (conducted with Caribbean island nations) and Strong Resolve 95 (a NATO maritime exercise)—to include peacekeeping training.

Tradewinds is a multiphased exercise, permitting the evaluation of both ground and maritime operations of U.S. and Caribbean forces. The exercise promotes readiness training for the regional forces in skills and missions identified by Caribbean political leaders. For instance, the 1993 exercise focused on disaster recovery activities, counterdrug operations, and small-unit tactics. Recent discussions among the Caribbean leaders identified the importance of peacekeeping and the possibility of their forces participating in such operations. The multiphase scenario approach of this exercise lends itself to peacekeeping training. To facilitate this, Tradewinds 94 will provide a new scenario phase to include the following:

- Crisis mediation between two contending factions.

- Arrangement of a cease-fire agreement.

- Employment of a composite military and police force to monitor the cease-fire.

- Employment of an election monitoring unit.

- Employment of both a military engineering and medical support unit to accomplish a humanitarian assistance project.
- Employment of a public affairs unit to publicize the "peacekeeping" exercise.
- Employment of a multinational joint command element.

The defense and police forces of the Caribbean nations are ideally suited for integration into a regional peacekeeping coalition force. The ground forces, coast guards, and police forces have a history of combined efforts. The Regional Security System (RSS) in the eastern Caribbean, for instance, actually integrates members of the police into a paramilitary special service unit that trains with other Caribbean defense forces, as well as with the armed forces of the United States, France, Great Britain, and the Netherlands. Also being evaluated is the option of including participants from government and nongovernment agencies in the Caribbean, and from other international organizations, to serve as "good office" negotiators, human rights monitors, election monitors, relief workers, and government reconstitution administrators. As restructured, Tradewinds 94 takes on greater relevance. It provides valid training in skills that enable the police and defense forces of the Caribbean nations to participate in regional or international peacekeeping efforts deemed appropriate by their own civilian leaders. Lessons learned during the Tradewinds 94 exercise will, in turn, be applied to the development of a scenario for NATO's Strong Resolve 95.

Strong Resolve is an exercise used to evaluate evolving maritime tactics and multinational operations. A proposal now under consideration for Strong Resolve 95 calls for a revised scenario that would require adapting the existing capability of an underway task force to meet an unforeseen "crisis" requirement. The proposed exercise would include activities in support of a simulated peacekeeping operation. Three options are feasible. First, a naval Construction Battalion (or "Seabee") Civic Action Team could be embarked as a planning cell for a humanitarian assistance project undertaken in support of a peacekeeping operation. Second, the onboard medical staff could be tasked to provide assistance to a multinational peacekeeping force deployed under a UN mandate. Third, the entire task force could participate in a peacekeeping scenario, to include providing "neutral territory" aboard the command vessel, where representatives from the parties in conflict may meet for supervised negotiations; accompanying neutral shipping in and out of a danger area adjacent to territories of the parties in a conflict; and monitoring and enforcing economic sanctions mandated by the UN Security Council.[5] Potentially, this exercise could require government and nongovernment participants for role-playing as mediators, negotiators from the contending factions, the civilian special representative of the UN secretary-general, and the military field commander of the peacekeeping force.

Additional consideration should be given to two follow-on options for Strong Resolve 95. First, ships from non-NATO countries in the selected exercise areas could be integrated into the peacekeeping phase of operations. This would exercise the task force's ability to integrate its capabilities with ad hoc coalition partners. Second, the peacekeeping phase of the scheduled exercise, if properly coordinated and approved, could take place "out of theater." With NATO's 1993 approval of the UN's request for assistance in enforcing the Bosnian no-fly zone, the out-of-theater barrier has been crossed. Again, we could maximize the utility of an existing exercise by adapting it in this case to new requirements confronting members of the alliance.

Other options exist for training and exercise support. The National Defense University (NDU) and the Intermediate and Advanced Service Colleges could reengineer applicable courses in order to provide training and research opportunities designed to familiarize officers with mediation, conflict resolution, and national reconstruction operations. The objective of such efforts would not be to train officers in how to conduct peacekeeping operations; rather, the goal would be to provide them with a broad outline of the organizations involved in peacekeeping operations and the role of the UN.

The Inter-American Defense Board (IADB) could develop a multinational command course to prepare senior officers of the militaries and defense forces in the Western Hemisphere for peace-enabling operations. The initial requirement, in this instance, is for the IADB to identify the particular skills required to command and control a multinational task force. Working on the basis of this information, the IADB could develop a course to acquaint senior officers with the particular skills needed for peace-enabling operations. The use of computer simulations would provide a practice field for overall evaluations.

In the alliance context, the NATO Defense College in Rome and the NATO school in Oberammergau could provide training programs for peace-enabling operations. The training familiarization provided by these schools could focus on mediation, conflict resolution, and national reconstruction operations. Such steps would be another practical measure to assist cooperation partners in preparing for potential peace-enabling missions.

International command-post exercises could be devised to evaluate the interface capabilities of the existing communication networks utilized by the UN, regional security alliances (such as NATO), national military command centers of UN member states, and transnational organizations involved in relief and assistance efforts. Communications are a crucial requirement for successful peace-enabling efforts at virtually every level. Global communication networks already exist; the objective here is to test how effectively these networks can be interlinked. On the basis of such tests and evaluations a communication network data base can be created, providing the UN or regional security alliances a single-point document for use during actual conflict resolution operations.

Finally, providing a facility for training and exercising designated forces could assist the UN in preparing for peace-enabling missions. Existing training ranges and computer simulators available within the United States and the NATO countries offer a large number of potential practice fields to train core elements of militaries willing to participate in defense coalitions. This would be the first step in establishing a needed baseline for peacekeeping and peace-enforcing skills. Emphasis would be placed on developing a core element capable of returning to their own national militaries and passing on acquired skills. During regional exercises, the skills acquired could be evaluated, tested, and validated.

Even more important is assuring sufficient training opportunities for the command elements of participants in peace-enabling missions. In both the United States and NATO long-established programs regularly provide training for senior officers. A training facility dedicated to similar goals exists at the Military Academy of the Russian General Staff. These mature and professional programs could be opened to the senior leadership of those nations willing to become participants in collective security coalitions.

Professional competence and command abilities are essential for effective peacekeeping and peace-enforcing operations. Accordingly, we need to assist our allies, friends, and partners in building the necessary expertise within their own ranks. American, Russian, and NATO contributions in this area are indispensable.

Support Infrastructure and Force Contributions

The importance of mediation and crisis resolution missions has been highlighted by recent events. Such operations require the identification of available and ready forces, the deployment of those forces to trouble spots, and a logistics system that can provide such forces sufficient support. The United States, the NATO allies, and Russia have resources and expertise to support such multinational undertakings. Specific contributions could include the use of existing C⁴I² infrastructure to facilitate multinational command and control; the use of national and alliance logistical capabilities to provide needed support services to multinational coalitions; highly trained and proficient command cells and military units, which can serve as observers, mediators, combat forces, and command elements for multinational coalitions; national and alliance air, ground, and maritime forces that can support UN-sanctioned missions through their presence, their surveillance, and the enforcement of sanctions and no-fly zones.

While each of these contributions is important, a particular element of the C⁴I² infrastructure—the collection and communication of information and intelligence—demands special emphasis. The technological edge of the United States and other major powers provides a broad range of capabilities that can provide a decisive advantage to multinational coalitions assembled for nearly any mission. The space-based systems of the United States and Russia, for example, can provide the UN-designated civilian special representative or military field commander the real-time intelligence needed to conduct operations and activities in a highly fluid situation. During the Gulf War, the U.S. Central Command and coalition forces were provided with an accurate depiction of the movement of all Iraqi forces. While the "fog of war" has not totally disappeared, it can be effectively penetrated. For less time-sensitive situations, the intelligence and information-gathering capabilities of the United States, Russia, and the alliance nations can provide the data needed to conduct routine coalition activities. Of particular interest to coalition leaders is data on such questions as the following: What are the capabilities and resources of assigned coalition partners? What are the capabilities and resources of contending factions? What are the political, economic, cultural, social, ethnic, and religious elements that could affect a given operation? What national infrastructure is available to support relief and recovery operations? And lastly, what global, regional, and national logistical capabilities are available to assist coalition activities? While hardly exhaustive of the information sought by decision makers in the field, this list is illustrative of the variety of data a military operational commander or a civilian special representative must have ready at hand—and which the global information network can provide. Rather than attempt to recreate a new C⁴I² infrastructure, the UN should consider seriously the use of the extensive capabilities already in existence.

Two as yet unfulfilled requirements merit special consideration as we move toward developing a logistics and C⁴I² infrastructure supportive of peace-enabling missions. First, a database of existing capabilities that could be contributed by national governments, private industry, and international organizations must be developed. Similarly, a catalog of C^4I^2 capabilities available to be contributed from existing national and regional command headquarters should be assembled. The early identification of potential contributors in either of these categories would facilitate the rapid deployment and employment of assigned forces—in situations where the speed of a response is often crucial in determining its effectiveness.

Support Doctrine

On the basis of the foregoing, it is evident that we will soon confront a pressing need for combined force packages of military, police, and civilian capabilities to respond to regional and international conflict resolution operations. Concurrently, as has been discussed, there is a requirement for fully trained combined operations commanders furnished with a C^4I^2 capability sufficient to provide a clear and accurate tactical picture, as well as the ability to direct and control all phases of a contingency operation. This composite force should be prepared to achieve the assigned objective of any stabilization, mediation, and crisis resolution operation.

To facilitate such operations, clearly articulated joint and combined doctrine—essential to providing guidance on a range of issues to both command elements and to the packages of capabilities assigned to them—is required. In this instance, the United States and NATO can contribute established doctrine, concept plans, and rules of engagement—developed for the coordination of multinational operations—that can be adapted to the requirements of ad hoc coalitions.

The U.S. Joint Staff has been preparing a series of three documents that are of particular relevance to this requirement. The first is *Joint Doctrine for Military Operations Other Than War* (Joint Publication 3–07), which addresses modes of applying existing military capabilities to the problems of providing assistance to civil authorities, conducting forward presence and show-of-force missions, undertaking combat operations associated with short-duration interventions, and carrying out postconflict restoration operations. The specific military operations encompassed by the short-of-war category include support to insurgencies and counterinsurgencies, counterterrorism operations, peacekeeping operations, and Defense Department support to counterdrug operations.[6]

The second document is *Joint Tactics, Techniques, and Procedures for Peacekeeping Operations* (Joint Publication 3–07.3). This document provides specific guidance for a number of components essential to peacekeeping operations, including command and control, planning and employment considerations, training requirements, and support functions. The third document, *Joint Doctrine for Peace-Enforcing Operations*, is in the initial stage of development. As a trilogy, these documents will form a corporate body of information representing an enormous investment of effort in studying and planning for the challenges of supporting stabilization, mediation, and crisis resolution operations. For its part, the NATO staff is developing an alliance document—Military Committee (or MC) Document 327, *Military Planning Document for NATO Support to Peacekeeping*. This document will provide a planning and employment framework for NATO participation in UN or Organization on Security and Cooperation in Europe (OSCE) peacekeeping operations.

A Unified Command and Control Network

The identification of a clear chain of authority is critical to the success of any peace-enabling effort. Yet, as noted recently by UN Under Secretary-General Marrack Goulding, "[E]xisting structures in New York have found it increasingly difficult to plan, command and control the greatly increased peacekeeping activities of recent years."[7] The fact of the matter is that basic shortcomings have been identified, in the findings of after-action reports and staff studies, in the ways in which the UN is organized for peace-enabling missions. For instance, the UN Headquarters in New York has a limited C^4I^2 infrastructure. Only recently has a crisis action center with operations twenty four hours a day been established. The secretary-general has no supporting crisis action staff, and the military planning staff is inadequately manned. The intermediate leadership level is not fully developed. Remarkably, despite these difficulties, peacekeeping missions currently operate in places ranging from El Salvador in Latin America to Angola, Somalia, and Mozambique on the African continent, throughout the Middle East and southwestern Asia, to Cambodia in Southeast Asia. The point to stress is that all such operations must be run more effectively and more efficiently. There is a real potential that the capabilities of the UN may be dangerously overextended as field operations expand (involving upwards of thirty thousand personnel), and costs balloon to hundreds of millions of dollars per mission on the average. In the midst of these challenges, member states are cutting defense budgets and reducing force levels. The UN is no less constrained than its members (indeed, given its dependence on contributed forces, it is perhaps *more* constrained) by the reality of finite security resources. Confronted with growing demands for peace-enabling missions, the UN may find the adaptive force package

concept a key part of matching declining resources to increasing requirements. Yet regardless of the type of force package deployed, an identified
command network is a necessary condition for success.

A chain of authority is not just a leadership hierarchy or a matrix showing
relationships between interconnected command headquarters. It is also (and
more importantly) a varied collection of people in possession of capabilities
directed toward a common purpose.

LEADERSHIP IN A TRANSNATIONAL WORLD

The cases of Somalia and the former Yugoslavia have demonstrated that
disorder in the international system increases if the forces of political
fragmentation and social upheaval are left to themselves. Whether in the
form of outside mediation or support for implementing a peace settlement,
action is required if change is to be shaped and directed in ways that will
promote peace, justice, prosperity, and democracy. Common sense suggests
that the response made to a given occurrence of disorder is dependent upon
the situation. In some instances, mediation is suitable; others require
peacekeeping activities. The most catastrophic situations may require tough
peace-enforcing actions. Disorder can be so mercurial that a crisis may
descend precipitously into a Hobbesian world in which innocent people
confront "continual fear and danger of violent death; and the life of man
[is] solitary, poor, nasty, brutish, and short."[8]

National governments and international organizations are increasingly
recognizing that a division of labor based on organizational expertise,
comparative technological advantage, and professional competence is essential for taming the political maelstrom we face today. The requirement
now is to give shape to a security "grid" that can identify, connect, and
channel the capabilities of national, regional, and international organization. By being able to shift patterns and relationships within such a grid, we
can ensure no one system is overloaded. In the present era of turbulence and
uncertainty, the establishment of such a system depends ultimately upon
effective leadership. For leadership to be effective, five elements are
essential:

- *Authority*: The moral strength and firmness of vision that engender respect from
  allies, partners, and opponents.
- *Confidence*: The courage of conviction and the political will to act in support of
  a national commitment.

- *Credibility*: The perception by allies, partners, and opponents that commitments made will be commitments kept.

- *Capabilities*: The forces, facilities, infrastructure, and expertise necessary to carry through on commitments to assist allies, deter opponents, and defend national interests.

- *Resources*: The fiscal funding to provide the capabilities—diplomatic, economic, and military—needed to support and sustain national commitments.

The first step in building our approach to the challenges of a new security environment is to recognize that the United States—uniquely in the post–Cold War world—offers all of these qualities. It was the United States, for example, that facilitated the creation of the monitoring group mounted by the Economic Community of West African States (known as ECOMOG) to carry out a peacekeeping effort in Liberia. It was the United States that built the coalition that expelled Iraq from Kuwait. It was the United States that provided a multimillion dollar assistance package to help Salvadoran soldiers make the transition to civilian life. And it was the United States that took the lead in creating a multinational response that tried to stem deteriorating conditions in Somalia.

Of course, the scale of global turbulence requires more than one leader. No one nation can—or should—serve as the world's policeman. What is the potential that other leadership centers might emerge? Certainly our former superpower rival remains a major player in the diplomatic and military arenas. In choosing democracy, Russia has now taken on the tremendous task of political and economic reconstruction.[9] Most of the republics of the former Soviet Union are turning inward as they contend with a broad range of political, economic, social, and ethnic problems. The Russian Federation itself faces many of these same challenges. While lacking the full range of resources and the scale of capabilities required, Russia can concentrate her capabilities to make real and effective contributions toward the enhancement of global security. Already the new leadership in Moscow has demonstrated a willingness to make contributions of substance; today we see a Russian peacekeeping presence in the Persian Gulf, in Yugoslavia and in former republics of the Soviet Union.

America's major economic competitors, Japan and Germany, lack the expeditionary military capability to engage in a full range of activities outside their own territorial borders (or in the particular case of Germany, outside alliance borders). Some observers also question whether Japan and Germany have the requisite political will to act. The Japanese people traditionally have opposed the deployment of their defense forces, even in support of UN peacekeeping operations. Nevertheless, the Japanese government has announced, in a recent policy statement, its intention to send fifty military personnel to Mozambique to join an ongoing UN peacekeeping operation; this was in fact carried out. In the German case, military personnel from the Bundeswehr are participating in the airdrop of food and humanitarian supplies to Bosnia in Operation Provide Promise, and in the airlift of crucial support to Sarajevo, as part of the UN humanitarian assistance effort. A recent decision of Germany's Constitutional Court cleared the way for German crews participate in NATO AWACS flights in support of the UN-mandated no-fly zone in Bosnia, Operation Deny Flight.[10] It is important to note that both the Japanese and German military roles are circumscribed by their constitutions—constitutions that are a product of the post-World War II reconstruction period.[11]

The People's Republic of China (PRC), while already a global political player, has the potential to play an even greater role in international politics.[12] Poised for an economic takeoff, the PRC is still struggling with the conflicting demands of a communist political system and an evolving free enterprise system. It seems fairly safe to forecast that the PRC will figure as one of the centers of global leadership in the next century. The question remains, however, whether Beijing will be a leading competitor or a leading partner.

Among other nations of the world, there are several that can be classified as dominant regional powers. But regional power does not translate automatically into a position of preeminent leadership capable of promoting large collective-security coalitions.

Indeed, the future may see the decline of nation-states as the dominant organizational feature of the international environment. Increasingly, international and nongovernmental organizations are challenging the traditional prerogatives of national governments. Certainly the UN holds the potential to be a far more significant force for promoting both stability and development. At the moment, the UN lacks the fiscal resources and internal command infrastructure to translate its emerging authority into effective leadership.

Even the alliance—with its combined credibility, capabilities, and resources—at times lacks the consensual political will to act outside its proscribed Cold War boundaries, especially when "windows of opportunity" are narrow and the time for decision is short. While pointing out that there is a consensus within NATO which supports an active alliance role in promoting stability in Central and Eastern Europe and in contributing to

conflict management, Manfred Wörner, NATO's late secretary-general, has
also observed:

Our resources seem abundant but our policy is less clear; and force—albeit on a
lower scale—may well have to be used. To intervene or not to intervene? If so,
when, where and how? And at what cost? It is hardly surprising that these dilemmas
are today taxing the moral and political resources of the democracies in a way quite
unknown during the Cold War.[13]

Though arriving at a consensus may involve difficult and deliberate negotiations, once a decision is reached the weight of the alliance's capabilities
can be brought to bear on resolving a crisis. The crux of Secretary-General
Wörner's observation is that the strength of NATO lies in the democratic
traditions of its members, and its consensual approach to security.

The changed security environment—and the absence of other states able
to exert the full scope of leadership—requires continued American engagement as a stabilizing force. The United States can and should encourage the
development of capabilities on the part of other nations, regional organizations, and the UN to assume greater leadership roles. In order to fulfill their
potential roles, emerging centers of leadership must be able to organize,
conduct, and complete operations against breaches of the peace and acts of
aggression. A greater number and wider variety of potential leadership
centers will substantially increase the responsiveness of the international
community to incipient crises.

AN UPDATED PEACE-ENABLING PARADIGM

Now, here, you see, it takes all the running you can do, to keep in the
same place. If you want to get somewhere else, you must run at least
twice as fast as that.
Lewis Carroll, *Through the Looking-Glass* (1872)

Together, measures discussed here form the core of a new approach to
global security building. The challenge is to integrate these proposals, and
recent lessons learned, into the framework of international stabilization,
mediation, and crisis resolution activities. Of course, there are obstacles to
such reform: the inertia of old habits, the entrenchment of international
bureaucracies, and the difficulty of reaching a multinational consensus on
strategic and tactical responses to breaches of the peace. When running at
least twice as fast only gets one further behind, there is a definite possibility

that a good solution is being applied to the wrong problem. Thus, in peacekeeping as traditionally understood—as with other security related discussions—the question emerges: is the operative paradigm still relevant?

This is an important question. A paradigm shapes the way we look at a particular situation. It sets down the reference points from which we survey current problems and future challenges. An outmoded paradigm can be dangerously misleading—distorting any evaluation of needed reforms. In discussions of UN stabilization, mediation, and conflict resolution activities, one paradigm shapes most views of peacekeeping. While the picture it presents is clear and easily understood, the image it presents is wrong. First, it does not reflect the complete range of diplomatic strategies—constructive, preventive, and persuasive—that can be employed to prevent, contain, or resolve a conflict.[14] Second, activities and operations used to implement these different strategies are not limited to just the two categories of peacekeeping and peace enforcing. There are numerous peace-enabling options currently in use by national policy makers and international organizations, running the full spectrum from precrisis peace-promoting activities to postconflict peace-building operations. Third, the UN may not be the principal actor. Faced with the difficulties of getting member states to commit forces—and the sometimes lengthy arguments over command and control of those forces—others may find themselves compelled to act in the absence of a UN consensus. Even should a consensus be achieved, member states may determine for themselves that the conditions for success are absent, or that the UN mandate and prescribed rules of engagement are inadequate. In such a case, it is likely that no action would be taken by anyone.

A more accurate depiction of international stabilization, mediation, and crisis resolution activities is feasible. Changes in the existing paradigm of peace-enabling efforts are suggested by a much broader array of challenges facing the UN and the international community. A changed paradigm should serve as the starting point for debating the evolving role of the UN as an enabling organization which would marshal the capabilities made available and the international community of responsible nations. The key operative word is capabilities. It implies more than the assignment of military combat and support units; beyond this, it recognizes the need for the contribution of such specially skilled personnel as translators, police forces, election monitors, and health care specialists.

A careful review of current UN peacekeeping operations reveals an unmistakable conclusion: the changed realities and new opportunities brought by the end of the Cold War compel us to move beyond the current paradigm of peace enabling. Of principal importance among the changed realities are an increasingly transnational world, in which national borders are more and more permeable to the flow of ideas, commerce, and people— as well as challenges and problems; transnational institutions addressing global issues, neither bounded nor controlled by national governments; national and regional crises assuming an international character through such acts of terrorism, kidnapping, hostage taking, and killing or threatening foreign nationals;[15] and crises and conflicts prompted by the gathering forces of political fragmentation, social upheaval, and virulent nationalism. A new set of requirements emerges from these changed realities. The need for strategic military assets is decreasing. Regional crises, which challenge local politico-military balances, appear more frequently. The demand for humanitarian relief and peacekeeping operations is increasing. The security environment is so dynamic that there are often only narrow opportunities for taking constructive action. The difficulty of responding to these new requirements with institutions and forces developed in a previous era was characterized quite adroitly by Marshal Yevgeny Shaposhnikov, commander of Commonwealth of Independent States (CIS) forces, at a recent North Atlantic Cooperation Council meeting: "Today is too early," Shaposhnikov observed, "but tomorrow is too late."

But the end of Cold War has presented us with the opportunity to develop new approaches to national defense and collective security. First, the evolving partnership between the former antagonists of the Cold War can facilitate both greater cooperation and collaboration in dealing with the full range of global challenges. Second, emerging leadership hubs—the UN, NATO, OSCE, and other regional associations—can promote collective security regimes built upon shared responsibilities and shared accountability.[16]

In designing a new conflict resolution framework, we must recognize that the world has confronted us with a broadening gray area between the classical definitions of peacekeeping and peace enforcing. Operations within this gray area must be guided by principles fundamental to all peacekeeping operations: mutual respect between the parties to the conflict and the peacekeeping organization, impartiality and neutrality toward the parties in the dispute, limits on the use of force, and transparency of operation to all parties in the dispute.

Beyond this, however, gray-area missions highlight shortcomings in the UN ability to respond: the absence of effective command and control infrastructure at the New York headquarters, the lack of sufficient fiscal resources, and the potential for overextension of capabilities. The UN is now placed in the tough position of having its credibility challenged in peacekeeping operations, while being haunted by its inability to deal effectively with peace-enforcing operations. It is, in short, a lose-lose situation. In finding a way out, the UN must undertake a sweeping assessment of the comparative advantages that various national governments, regional alliances, and international organizations can bring to stabilization, mediation, and conflict resolution efforts.

The facts indicate that, while the UN may have a broad competence for classical peacekeeping operations, national forces and regional defense alliances enjoy a comparative advantage in the command and control of sophisticated military operations. This study has noted the wealth of existing capabilities that could be provided by the United States, Russia, and the NATO alliance to UN peace-enabling missions. National and alliance capabilities are tools needed for implementing the full range of missions inherent in an paradigm built upon the framework of constructive, preventive, and persuasive strategies.[17]

In undertaking these missions, national and alliance capabilities should be fully integrated into the framework of UN-sponsored activities when a collective decision for action has been taken. As stated by former NATO Secretary-General Wörner:

We have to develop in Europe, as elsewhere, the mandates and the capabilities of regional organizations. This approach is wholly consistent with the UN Charter. We must therefore bring the available structures—NATO, WEU, EC, CSCE and UN—into a coordinated pattern of cooperation.[18]

Where a UN consensus does not exist, a consensus for action (and the ability to act) might exist in other organizations or ad hoc coalitions. Such an option cannot—and should not—be dismissed.

The UN—both the institution as a whole and its separate agencies—possesses unique capabilities for stabilization, mediation, and conflict resolution efforts. As a spokesman for the community of responsible nations, the UN carries an aura of authority untainted by national interests. Consequently, the UN can assert the claim of neutrality and impartiality required for mediation efforts. As the organizer for collective responses to breaches of the peace, the UN has a recognized right to authorize the full range of diplomatic, economic, and military actions to restore the peace. These two roles—mediator and enforcer—do not coexist in a single agency of the UN. The mediator role resides in the Office of the Secretary-General; the enforcement role is exercised by the Security Council. This bifurcation is both appropriate and useful; it can serve as the basis for a new approach to undertaking the expanded range of peace-enabling missions.

In the midst of the Cold War's ideological struggle, the Office of the Secretary General developed and undertook mediation and peacekeeping missions in response to a critical need. Through difficult experience, it became evident that essential to the success of such missions are unquestioned integrity, professionalism, and impartiality in the person of the secretary-general and designated representative. But while the secretary-general had to remain above the fray, the Security Council is empowered by the Charter to take collective action against breaches of the peace. Collective security requires leadership in all its basic elements: authority, confidence, credibility, capabilities, and resources.[19] With the end of the Cold War, the Security Council's authority, confidence, and credibility are emerging unmistakably. But providing a budget and force structure sufficient to undertake enforcement operations remains a problem.

For four decades, mediation and peacekeeping missions were conducted by the secretary-general. The record shows measured success. When a willingness to negotiate existed among contending factions, the secretary-general was usually able to achieve a settlement (e.g., in the cases of Indonesian, Congolese, and Namibian independence, and national reconciliation in El Salvador). When settlement was not possible, the secretary-general typically sought to arrange for a cease-fire that contained the conflict (e.g., Kashmir, the Sinai and Golan Heights, and the Western Sahara). It is perhaps safe to suggest that the problems now being encountered in such ongoing peacekeeping operations as Angola, Bosnia-Herzegovina, Cambodia, and Somalia result from the secretary-general's movement into the gray area of peace enforcing. By entering the fray—in contravention of its established role—the secretary-general's office becomes a target of criticism. Secretary-General Boutros-Ghali was verbally and physically attacked during inspection trips to UN operations in Bosnia, Cambodia, and Somalia in early 1993.

It is inappropriate and self-defeating for one agency to simultaneously conduct peacekeeping and peace-enforcement operations—even if that one agency is the Office of the Secretary-General of the UN. Doing so taints the secretary-general's aura of impartiality and neutrality for fact-finding, mediation, and peacekeeping activities. It obfuscates the functional difference between peacekeeping and peace enforcing. It creates confusion over accountability by complicating the lines of command and control. And, most dangerous of all, it undermines the secretary-general's necessary role in postconflict reconstruction and reconciliation. Hence it is necessary to delineate clearly the scope and substance of peacekeeping and peace-enforcing missions.

In an updated peace-enabling paradigm, the role of mediator and peacekeeper would be retained by the Office of the Secretary-General—the appropriate decision center for assessing where and when classical peacekeeping operations can be accomplished. The criteria upon which such an assessment must be based are straightforward: both sides in a dispute must agree to a cease-fire protocol; they must be willing to abide by the settlement; and they must respect the neutrality of UN Blue Helmet forces. If the proper conditions do not exist, a peacekeeping mission should not be undertaken. Much the same argument can be made for postenforcement operations; the secretary-general should be responsible for reconstruction and reconciliation efforts. Here again, the Office of the Secretary-General would have to make the political determination that a given situation is suitable for such UN operations, on the basis of the criteria of engagement for peacekeeping suggested above.

In instances where significant breaches of the peace exist, the Security Council, and not the secretary-general, should serve as the facilitator for a collective security response. There should be a threshold of violence the crossing of which must automatically prompt an international response. Possible trip wires include the potential for escalation beyond the borders of the actual dispute, documented cases of genocide, and conditions of civil war. It must be remembered that intervention in a crisis is a political decision, to be made by civilian decision makers. Quite properly, the determination of whether the threshold has been crossed belongs with the civilian political leadership of the international community. A Security Council resolution thus expresses an international consensus on the United Nations' use of force—including lethal force.

The UN Charter provides a mechanism for making forces available to the Security Council. This mechanism, however, has never been implemented—and if implemented, would not provide an appropriate command and control infrastructure for sophisticated enforcement operations. Rather than placing forces under the command of the Security Council, a different concept is required—a collective security compact. Under such a concept, based upon the Lockean idea of the social contract, the community of responsible nations would join together to respond to significant breaches of the peace and acts of aggression.[20] Such actions could be undertaken by a multinational unified task force (as in Operation Desert Storm)—or by a competent regional alliance (as in Operation Deny Flight in Bosnia). In both instances, the Security Council would provide a mandate authorizing such action. This is the more appropriate role for the Security Council—authorizing, not conducting, operations. There remains a gray area in which significant force might be required for a peacekeeping operation. The need for combat-capable forces should be an early criterion in determining whether a protective or preventive peacekeeping operation would be assigned to the secretary-general or be part of a collective security compact. Unfortunately, the boundary demarcating one set of cases from the other is uncertain, and will likely remain so. Ultimately, each such decision rests with the leaders of the member states of the UN. Extreme cases, however, can be easy to identify. Somalia is a recent example. The scale of violence and disorder in that country was so great that the UN Blue Helmet force itself, deployed as the United Nations Organization in Somalia (UNOSOM), was brutalized by the warring factions. Even more shocking, the humanitarian assistance supplies the UN force was assigned to protect continued to be confiscated by rival tribes as part of the resource denial strategy pursued by all sides. As the situation became more catastrophic, and more frequently reported by the media, the Security Council approved Operation Restore Hope—in essence, a unified task force effort to assist in the delivery of humanitarian relief and to restore some semblance of order in Somalia.[21]

The situation in Bosnia-Herzegovina also fits the same mold—a war in which the shelling of playgrounds, the rape of women, and the destruction of entire communities are treated as routine acts of war. The tragic dilemma in the Bosnian case is that, other than accepting the territorial conquests of over a year of ethnic cleansing, the options available toward stopping the violence could well prove counterproductive, escalating the conflict and worsening the violence.

When a collective response to a significant breach of the peace is required, one possible authorizing instrument would be a Security Council mandate. (Again, the option of regional or unilateral action remains viable—and cannot be precluded.) The Security Council mandate would specify the mission objectives, the scope of the operation, approval procedures for ROE, and the criteria for mission success. This last requirement would provide the measure for judging how well a mission was progressing, and when it had reached completion. For an enforcement operation, the Security Council would request a competent regional alliance to undertake the operation or solicit a competent military power to organize and lead a unified task force. The task force, in turn, would organize and provide the capabilities package required to enforce the Security Council mandate.[22] In assuming enforcement obligations under a collective security compact, a nation or regional grouping would enjoy an inherent right to negotiate the terms of reference. Such flexibility ensures complete understanding by all parties of the mission objectives and mission parameters. It is the responsibility of either the regional alliance or the commander of the task force (as the case may be) to command and complete the assigned mission while ensuring minimal casualties among deployed forces.

Of course, an element of national interest enters into the equation in virtually any peace-enforcing mission.[23] In democratic states, the decision to send the nation's military forces into harm's way must be based on the political will to act, supported by a consensus within the political leadership and among the public. Nations or alliances will agree to act—and the public will support such actions—only if their best interests are seen to be served by containing a crisis or achieving the pacific resolution of a conflict. Thus, the determinative influence of national interest should not be regarded as a hindrance; rather, properly channeled, it is the paramount consideration that will propel collective security from theory to practice.

In undertaking a UN-mandated enforcement operation, command and control are crucial. Many complaints involving ongoing UN field operations have centered on this issue.[24] The peace-enabling paradigm proposed by this study suggests a different command structure. In enforcement operations conducted by a regional alliance or a unified task force, a Security Council resolution provides the mission statement. The regional alliance or unified task force determines the command structure, force requirements, and logistic requisites. Command would be determined, most likely, by the relative degree of capability contributed to a unified task force operation, or by existing command and control arrangements within an existing defense alliance. In all instances, overall command for a deployed force remains with national authorities; operational control resides with the intermediate command level; and tactical command belongs with the field commander. Similar command structures operated in Somalia (with the U.S.-led unified task force), in Liberia (with the Nigerian-led ECOMOG force), and in the skies over Bosnia (with the NATO operation in support of the no-fly zone).

The point to make is that there are existing military structures having the expertise, capabilities, and proven track record required for conducting enforcement operations. Using and adapting what exists is more effective and efficient than having the UN create a new, untested system. The updated peace-enabling paradigm and its associated command and control infrastructure proposed here represent one possible option.

This study, and the paradigm it develops, is intended to serve as a point of departure for further discussions—discussions that can promote a more viable security framework. With the end of the Cold War, we hold an unexpected opportunity to shape a new world where nations freely choose democracy, where tolerance is the norm, where a preference for market systems ensures economic growth and opportunity, and where governments and peoples are committed to settling differences peacefully. This opportunity will not come again in our lifetimes; indeed, it may be unique in human history. However, challenges and threats to this emerging order still exist. The world has not seen the end of evil, and the sources of conflict in this new era are too numerous for any one nation or alliance to underwrite global and regional stability. The solution is to promote collective security, by facilitating the creation, training, and exercising of appropriate forces for coalition building.

American leadership is required; yet it can neither be simply assumed nor merely asserted. Leadership must ultimately be demonstrated. Addressing cadets at West Point, President Bush observed: "Leadership requires formulating worthy goals, persuading others of their virtue, and contributing one's share of the common effort—and then some. Leadership takes time, it takes patience, it takes work." The time, patience, and work will have proved worth the effort if, at the end, we have helped to shape a democratic, prosperous, and just future. The goal is simple, but difficult to achieve: a shared vision, built upon a shared responsibility, to achieve a shared future.

NOTES

1. Alberto Coll, "America as the Grand Facilitator," *Foreign Policy* (Summer 1992): 51. Dr. Coll recently served as principal deputy assistant secretary for special operations and low-intensity conflict.

2. Coll, 54.

3. Information provided in *Presidents & Prime Ministers: International Perspectives from World Leaders, Asia Issue* (March–April 1993): 38.

4. *Joint Tactics, Techniques, and Procedures for Peacekeeping Operations* (Washington: The Joint Staff, Joint Publication 3–07.3, December 15, 1992), VI-6.

5. Ibid., I-16 and I-17.

6. *Joint Doctrine for Military Operations Other Than War* [Proposed], Joint Publication 3–07 (Washington: The Joint Staff, 1992), III-2.

7. Marrack Goulding, remarks at the Cyril Foster Lecture to the Examination School, Oxford University, March 4, 1993.

8. In *Leviathan*, his major political treatise, Thomas Hobbes observed that, in the absence of government, human beings would be in a state of war. Hobbes, born in 1588, lived through the English Civil War of the early seventeenth century. Being both a witness and victim of the political disorder of his age, Hobbes advocated an absolute form of government. Only if government illegally sought to take the life of one of its subjects did Hobbes argue that a citizen had the right to resist. The quote is taken from *Leviathan*, Part I, Chapter 13.

9. I was in Moscow March 14–16, 1993, meeting with senior military officers, foreign ministry officials, and the deputy chairman of the Committee on Defense and Security. During these discussions, the Russians were quite deliberate in affirming that they had chosen democracy for themselves.

10. The issue of German participation in AWACS flights in support of the UN no-fly zone in Bosnia-Herzegovina was brought before the Federal Constitutional Court by the Free Democratic Party, the junior partner in Chancellor Helmut Kohl's coalition government. Testifying before the Court, former NATO Secretary-General Manfred Wörner stated that if the German crew members left the planes "that they would harm the efficiency, the reputation, and the credibility of the Alliance." On April 8, 1993, the Court approved German participation. In its decision, the Court warned that continuing Germany's self-imposed restrictions on its military role would "endanger the trust for Germany within the [NATO] alliance."

11. In Japan's case, the 1992 International Peace Cooperation Law permits Japanese Self-Defense Forces to participate in overseas peacekeeping operations. The new law limits the number of personnel that can be deployed to two thousand, requires the approval of the Diet before any mission, prohibits the use of weapons except in self-defense, and requires a cease-fire in place before the dispatch of Japanese personnel. In the case of Germany, the two operative articles of the German *Grundgesetz*, or Basic Law (the German Constitution), seem to be contradictory. One states that the German military is intended for defensive purposes only; the other expressly permits Germany to join in international "collective security" coalitions. This reinforces the perception that the essential condition for German participation in international collective security efforts is the political will to act.

12. In recent collective-security decisions by the UN Security Council, the PRC has abstained. Thus, the Chinese have not specifically approved the UN action; by not exercising their veto right, however, they have made it possible for the UN to act. The PRC has acted in areas that affect core security interests; for example, Chinese peacekeeping troops are serving in Cambodia.

13. Manfred Wörner, remarks at the Munich Conference on Security Policy, February 7, 1993.

14. The three diplomatic strategies are addressed in a longer, unpublished version of this chapter, in sections entitled "Diplomacy and the Use of Assistance" and "Diplomacy and the Use of Force."

15. This assessment was made by Major General Olurin, a former ECOMOG field commander in Liberia, in a paper presented at a seminar in the United States.

16. As an example of expanding efforts in this area, the secretary-general of the Organization of African Unity proposed a conflict resolution strategy for that continent at an organizational meeting in June 1992. One specific proposal called for member states to earmark standby forces for contributions to peacekeeping operations.

17. For a complete description, see the previous section of this chapter, "A Proposed Blueprint for the Future."

18. Wörner, remarks at the Munich Conference on Security Policy, February 7, 1993.

19. For a complete description, see the earlier section "Leadership in a Trans-national World."

20. In his *Treatise on Government*, John Locke, a political philosopher of the seventeenth century, spelled out ideas of a basic social contract between the government and the governed. Locke's theories were incorporated into the U.S. Constitution.

21. Specific case studies of UN peacekeeping operations are provided in a longer unpublised version of this chapter.

22. The military capabilities package would include logistics, combat operations, engineer and medical support, and humanitarian and relief efforts. Private and civilian contributions—based upon separate need assessments—would be blended into the military field operations.

23. Case studies of unilateral and collective interventions are provided in a longer unpublished version of this chapter.

24. In a stinging assessment, Major General Lewis MacKenzie, former UN field commander in Bosnia-Herzegovina, has argued that there is no command and control system. Additionally, General MacKenzie observed that the civilian-contracted logistics system does not work, and that the UN uses budget constraints, rather than mission requirements, to determine equipment needed for deploying units.

Conclusion: In the Pursuit of Democracy and Security

DANIEL N. NELSON

DEMOCRACY AND "ESSENTIAL COMBINATIONS"

Democracy does not "happen." While its tenets are of unquestionable value for the quality of life within and among states, democracies never appear without extraordinary efforts by individuals such as Raúl Alfonsín, Liu Binyan, or Floribert Chebeya. And, even when courageous proponents of democracy enjoy moments of triumph, "times of trouble"—as Robert A. Dahl points out—almost inevitably lie ahead.

To individual and collective efforts, however, must be added much more. An arduous and lengthy trek awaits those who seek to implant democratic roots in anything other than the most fertile soil. The persistence of autocratic rule or party dictatorships in such cases as Zaïre and China, or the immense damage inflicted by the Argentine Junta, which used secret police repression and aggression in efforts to prolong its rule, have been amply demonstrated in this volume.

In the fabric of democracy are interwoven domestic and international conditions, individual and group actions, proximate causes and background environments. But, in contributions to *After Authoritarianism*, we have seen an *essential combination*: intense effort and sacrifice within societies afflicted by authoritarianism must be united with larger endeavors to ensure socioeconomic and external security. Simon Serfaty and Regina Karp have portrayed the dilemmas confronted by existing European security institutions as the continent's postcommunist eastern half struggles to achieve more democracy and less disorder; Charles William Maynes and Admiral Paul David Miller, using wide-angle approaches, articulate the diplomatic and military requisites for threat abatement strategies in coming years as the United States and its democratic partners strive to reduce the spread of ethnic conflict and other transnational perils.

Democracy, we find, can be nurtured only in environments without imminent threats that can otherwise be used by demagogues to enhance their appeal. Civil society and individual citizenship will not, our contributors suggest, make it to the democratic finish line absent both an international setting in which plural and competitive institutions and processes can be nurtured slowly *and* a sense of socioeconomic justice consistent with democratic values and procedures.

Today's plans and programs to assist or impart democratic institutions, processes, and values do not exhibit this understanding. Failing to understand that the genesis of democracy is intimately associated with citizenship and civil society in a milieu of security means that "democratization" will be misdirected and resources squandered on matters altogether ephemeral. And, as systemic performance on the domestic and international realms is perceived to deteriorate, enemies of democracy will gain strength.

O'Donnell and Schmitter, known for their work on transitions from authoritarianism, have observed that "the core principle of democracy is citizenship."[1] Indeed, it is axiomatic that democracy as we know it cannot exist without popular engagement in public life and a corresponding accountability of political leaders to the public. An alienated and distant public leaves the political sphere to those who arrogate power to a small clique, group, or class.

Intellectuals, workers, and others can recognize the essential role of nongovernmental activity in moving political life toward the open, tolerant, and plural standards of democracy. This is the *civil society*. Dissidents may be confronted by an implacable hold of autocrats or parties on formal positions of power; only by creating an alternative realm of civil society, divorced from those "in power," could the ferment of democracy find expression. And, in fact, the expansion of a public political realm can be successful, providing the principal impetus for the departure—in most cases, peacefully—of dictators or other autocratic rulers.[2]

But, what enables a society to develop and maintain an active public political sphere in which those holding state power are held accountable to the citizenry? And, what conditions endanger such a participatory culture and threaten public withdrawal, leaving political life to extremists and demagogues?

CIVIL SOCIETY, PARTICIPATORY CULTURE, AND PUBLIC LEGITIMATION

Democracy's promise has been coupled with a corresponding danger of disorder. Which of these directions postauthoritarian transitions takes is not a matter of political fate. The corner will be turned towards stable democracy only to the degree that an enlarged public political sphere is created and the norms of a participatory culture firmly and generally accepted.

Public legitimation and the accountability of those in power to citizens must often be generated outside electoral mechanisms, judicial procedures, or the bureaucracy. With those institutions and processes still in the control of an authoritarian clique, party, or junta, the extension of civil society is the harbinger of an expanded public political sphere. A "silent revolution" can occur incrementally, with disaffection spreading and nongovernmental organizations providing socioeconomic and even political alternatives to the ruling elite. And, lest we think that such a public, civil process is an artifact of one culture or region—that is, tied to one "civilization" vis-à-vis others—we need only to see the similarity among Chinese, Argentines, Zaïreans, or Eastern Europeans in their reliance on "the people," their awareness, and their courage.

Other views of democratic transitions offer very different emphases. Samuel Huntington is among those who have argued for a procedural definition of democracy, that is, regularized, competitive elections.[3] Structures and processes, however, are not self-generating. Although the presence or absence of competitive elections, functioning parliaments, and other accouterments may signal democracy, they do not create it.

The transformation of political life toward a plural, participatory democracy depends, ultimately, on citizenship. And, citizenship is not a matter of procedure and institutional roles as much as it is an artifact of culture, comprised of attitudes, norms, and expectations. As the public political realm expands, replacing intraparty and ideological limitations, citizens become "legitimators" with expectations for responsive political institutions and leaders.[4]

Unfortunately, we neither understand this process well *nor* know how to prevent a weakening of public legitimation. As citizens' own expectations for their problems to be solved and their needs to be met exceed capacities of new governments, an erosion of citizen's trust in institutions and leaders can begin anew. Interwoven with such an attitudinal detachment will be, invariably, an abandonment of the public political sphere—a purposeful apathy that means not voting, not paying attention to political events, and turning away from other associational activities.

What is it that citizens as participants want, need, and expect from postauthoritarian systems? What are the greatest dangers to the fragile legitimacy bequeathed to the first generations of postauthoritarian governments? What can be done to mitigate those perils, and thereby to avoid a public detachment from, or even abandonment of, the postauthoritarian public sphere?

To these questions, our volume has offered no *a priori* answers. Yet, as we see many citizens willing to relinquish goals of plural, competitive democracies for the assurances of renewed authoritarianism and responsive to demagogic appeals more than to the responsibilities of participating themselves, the urgency of these questions becomes clear.

We might be tempted to suspect that countries where repression was longest or most severe will have the greatest difficulty in democratic transitions *or* that cultural differences somehow predetermine democratic potential. This "clash of civilizations" way of thinking is both absurd cultural myopia and empirically wrong.

The troublesome prognosis for protodemocracies, then, must be explained by other factors. History and culture do not tell us why political behavior varies in the ways revealed by empirical data. And, other variables—ethnic composition or rate of economic growth, for example—help little. A largely homogeneous country with a growing economy may have lower participation rates and more public disaffection from political life than a rather heterogeneous state with continuing economic troubles. Unless one were prepared to accept the counterintuitive notion that fewer ethnic frictions and an improving economy are reasons to be politically dissatisfied, these commonly identified factors do not provide explanations.

An alternative hypothesis posits that the pace of economic change—particularly change that is perceived as too fast (i.e., "all shock, no therapy")—affects the prognosis for popular commitment to democratic processes; once a threshold of pain is crossed, no refinements in electoral procedure, due process, or plural media can compensate for diminished living standards.

This approach focuses on the social and political costs of accelerating a broad range of market-oriented reforms—ending centralized control of wages and prices, selling off state property, establishing the full convertibility of the national currency, and other steps.

In the United States, an intimate association between democracy and free markets is assumed. A rapid transition to private ownership, and a withdrawal of the state from economic decision making, are thought to imbue a sense of individual responsibility and entrepreneurial initiative. The right to own and to profit from ownership, plus the centrality of these rights to democratic republics, is thoroughly embedded in the eighteenth- and nineteenth-century liberalism that propelled early American political thought.

But today, "freemarketdemocracy" is contorted into a single expression, and applied with the vigorous enforcement of the International Monetary Fund (IMF) and other multilateral instruments. The prolonged evolution of capitalism and institutions of democratic republics that the United States (and a few other countries) were able to experience is not available to postauthoritarian states at the end of the twentieth century.

It is plausible that the forced march toward free market economies, notwithstanding the exports it may generate, the industrial surge it might create, or the Mercedes dealerships which it can spawn, fosters a milieu of socioeconomic insecurity. Further, such insecurity—perhaps exacerbated by cultural, ethnic, or other factors—may harm participation, commitment to tenets of tolerance, pluralism, and competition and other core elements of democratic citizenship.

Indeed, mounting empirical evidence suggests that citizens' commitment to participatory democracy suffers most in conditions of insecurity. A principal source of insecurity is economic—recognizing one's precarious economic condition relative to others, particularly if changes that could make things worse are being pursued quickly. Repeated studies have identified the strongly negative effect of income inequality on democratization.[5] Highly income-unequal societies, in other words, are not those that spawn or coexist with democracy.

To these broadly comparative findings we can now add limited but highly suggestive opinion data. Support for what we might term "democratic principles" (beliefs in the value of competitive elections, equal justice, and freedom to criticize the government) have been found (in Eastern Europe) to be positively associated with optimism about personal finances *or* general systemic optimism.[6]

Correspondingly, recent comparative research has concluded that the most important attitude for a system's democratic prognosis is a general public support for *gradual change*.[7] Rapid, externally enforced "marketization," accompanied by at least a temporary surge in income inequality, will *heighten* insecurity while *conflicting* with a preference for gradual change. This is a mix that bodes ill for protodemocracies.

To this source of insecurity, we can add new or worsening perils from within—for example, "freedom of action [that] has turned into defenselessness against criminals"[8] and interethnic tensions or conflict. External threats, too, can be perceived from mass migrations or direct attack.

The implications of such an association deserve immediate and in-depth exploration. If citizens' involvement in the public political sphere is weakened by a heightened sense of insecurity brought on by both external conditions (wars and turmoil) and unrelenting and wrenching internal changes, then the future of nascent democracies is "security dependent."

We need to question and reassess an initial emphasis on institutions and processes characteristic of Western democracies—for example, stressing laws that enable private ownership, skills for entrepreneurs, parliamentary and judicial professionalism, or the techniques of effective political campaigns. We are not yet sure, but have ample reason to suspect, that such an emphasis miss by a wide margin the needs which lie at the core of most individuals' participation in and commitment to a political system—needs for socioeconomic and physical security.

Free market economies coupled with democratic political institutions and processes are the conditions in which postauthoritarian countries *can* find peace and prosperity. The population's role in such a transition is essential. A democracy cannot exist where the public political sphere is weak or collapsing, for without such a participatory ethos there is no responsiveness or accountability. Yet, it may be unavoidable that postauthoritarian publics will turn away from new demands being placed upon them if the costs are perceived to be too high—if unemployment, inflation, crime, and political turmoil are threatening.

Group or individual political behavior required to obtain or cement the victory over authoritarianism—that is, civil society and participatory citizenship—are not yet sufficiently strong in cases such as China, Zaïre, or parts of postcommunist Europe. To maintain a robust public political sphere without reassurance about the security expected in or provided by a new, fledgling democracy is a dubious proposition. Were faltering postauthoritarian citizenship to be most strongly tied to popular fears which contribute to democracy's opponents, then the changes we promote must be linked to assurances and guarantees for safety and well-being. If civil society and citizenship after authoritarianism are not nurtured, then no fledgling democracy will long survive.

DEMOCRATIZATION POLICY

Focusing on the citizenry, not institutions or processes, implies a greater concern for the performance of a system in delivering "political goods" of central importance to individuals and their families—peace, security, and justice, for example.[9] This different portrait of postauthoritarian transitions is one derived from the "bottom up," looking first at what matters most to the most people.

Western funding agencies have given strong priority in their global activities to privatization; strengthening the professionalism of new parliaments, judiciaries, parties, and trade unions; and improving electoral and legislative processes.[10] These multiple assistance programs have sought to train and impart a model, not to understand or explain. To the degree that the role of citizens in unmaking authoritarianism and making democracy has been discussed, it has been assumed that Western support and encouragement are essential.

The perspectives offered in this volume should lead us to different conclusions. Citizens bring an end to authoritarian regimes through their disaffection, noncompliance, and (ultimately) velvet or violent revolution. A consistent failure of those engaged in democratization activities is to view such endeavors as *assistance* programs, in which Western experience is taught or imparted. Most often, privatization and democratization programs acknowledge little about the indigenous capacity of a country's population—as individuals acting alone or in association with one another—to insist on changes that call leaders to account and ensure the tenets of democracy.

By such an omission, and by making policies from Washington, D.C., Brussels, or other Western capitals, we ignore the importance to successful transitions of the behavior and values of those who live within a particular state. In the U.S. case, centralizing decision making in Washington has "complicated coordination and implementation of policy," while the American antipathy toward routing aid through governments has meant that coordination with host governments has been minimal.[11] But fundamental socioeconomic and political changes cannot be generated or consummated via external manipulation; the linchpin of democratic change is unquestionably an enlarged participation and heightened role for the populace, developing citizenship where previously the population was confined to the role of subjects.

In my view, we must move decisively away from the notion that a successful democratic transition can be merely transferred or transplanted, and into an exploration of democracy's dependence on an indigenous generation of citizenship.

Instead, we must ask how an expansion of the public political sphere can be generated with the power to topple authoritarian regimes with massive street demonstrations, not civil war. Conversely, we must consider dangers to that participatory ethos.

The answers, as implied above, lie in socioeconomic and external security. Where threats are perceived to exceed capacities to meet those threats, insecurity is present. Where people are insecure, the norms of democracy are unlikely to take root.

If postauthoritarian systems must, by virtue of international pressure, accelerate transformations to the point that income inequality rises and a desire for gradual change is violated, transitions will fail. Our goal is a successful movement to free markets and democratic systems, not necessarily rapid change. The incompatibility of these criteria is now evident.

Accepting slower socioeconomic change, expanding safety nets, eliminating foreign debt accumulated by prior dictatorships, opening Western markets—these are minimal steps by which to reduce domestically generated threats. Retargeting Western (G-7) support for postauthoritarian transitions toward enhancing the indigenous public political sphere is also essential. To some degree, the United States began to undertake such a reorientation in 1994 with the "Democracy Network Program" conceived by the Agency for International Development.[12] With $30 million, this AID initiative will not turn the tide. But, the concept is new and the emphasis appropriate. Helping nongovernmental organizations in democracy, environment, economic growth, and social safety net sectors via this small endeavor may slow the deterioration of civil society and citizenship in a region such as Eastern Europe. The weakening of the public political sphere, however, will continue to debilitate democratic transitions there and elsewhere until populations sense a heightened capacity to influence policy, to hold leaders accountable, and to assure jobs and social peace.

At an international level, the answer is also security. We have erred greatly by failing to establish means to abate threats in the Cold War's aftermath. Now more than ever, the threat-rich and capacity-poor regions of the world require not the extension of military alliances but the establishment of a robust regional collective-security organizations.

Security needs in most of the world's troubled regions will be best served through mechanisms for dispute arbitration, early-warning and observer missions, negotiation teams, and true peacekeeping forces (i.e., when there is a peace to keep)—not through an infusion of arms to balance power or through great power intervention. One very underfunded effort, headed by the OSCE's high commissioner for national minorities (now former Dutch Foreign Minister Max van der Stoel), exemplifies the enormous impact that such singular instruments can have in reducing threats and averting conflict. Far more resources and political support for such endeavors, housed within a collective organization, will be the only effective means by which to derive an external security for states in strife-prone regions.

Civil society gives birth to an expanded public political realm and the dawn of public legitimation. But that achievement can be endangered because of the costs of transition and external perils which undercut popular commitments to change and public patience with transition processes. The insecure withdraw, trying to protect themselves and their family, and recoil from public life. Once that begins to happen, the field of politics is left open to neoauthoritarians, or to the same people who inhabited prior regimes, albeit "reborn" with different labels.

Endangered by the perception of socioeconomic and international threats, group and individual engagement in the political sphere can be encouraged and protected only by abating those threats. Such domestic and external measures must be coupled with an assiduous effort to target Western support toward indigenous groups and citizens themselves. Encouraging entrepreneurial activities, providing legislatures with computerized voting procedures, enabling parties to produce superb television spots—these and other accouterments of democracy are meaningless unless government provides fundamental political goods to citizens. Indeed, without a strong, vibrant public political realm, where citizens act as legitimators, democracy will soon recede, and all-too-familiar authoritarianism will return with a vengeance.

SUMMARY

Opposing authoritarianism in Latin America, Eastern Europe, China, or sub-Saharan Africa requires the effort of individuals and groups as they spawn participatory citizenship and civil society. But, without a larger framework of socioeconomic and external security, the public political sphere and newfound accountability will erode and a time of troubles will ensue. These strong and omnipresent ties between postauthoritarian transitions and threats which confront people from internal or exogenous sources are the lessons of five years of post–Cold War experiences that form the core of this volume.

Even when they are revealed, the recognition of such complexities does not demarcate a clear path toward stable, prosperous democracy in any region. But we do know, unequivocally, that we cannot find and keep the benefits of a democracy without absorbing the costs of creating and defending it. These unsurprising, yet troubling reminders—that escaping authoritarianism is neither cheap nor easy—may be the consensual message of this book's contributors.

NOTES

1. Guillermo O'Donnell and Philippe Schmitter, *Transitions from Authoritarian Rule: Tentative Conclusions about Uncertain Democracies* (Baltimore: Johns Hopkins University Press, 1986), Chapter 2.

2. I have explored the expansion of the public political realm in European communist systems, leading toward the demise of communist party rule, in my chapter "The Rise of Public Legitimation in the Soviet Union and Eastern Europe."

3. Samuel Huntington in his *The Third Wave* (University of Oklahoma Press, 1993), Chapter 1, argues for a procedural definition of democracy based on the presence of elections. Even the most "free and fair" elections, however, do not ensure that access to political candidacy will be available to all, that policies pursued by the victor will be guided by tolerance and the rule of law, or that the international behavior of the elected government will follow peaceful relations with neighbors. Democracy, in other words, cannot be disassociated from who is elected, why they are elected, and what they do once they are elected.

4. Again, my chapter "The Rise of Public Legitimation in the Soviet Union and Eastern Europe" discusses these developments in detail.

5. One example is Edward N. Muller, "Democracy, Economic Development and Income Inequality," *The American Sociological Review* 53, no. 1 (1988): 50–68; Muller's citations include numerous other studies with related findings.

6. Mary E. McIntosh, Martha Abele MacIver, and Daniel G. Abele, "Publics Meet Market Democracy in Central and Eastern Europe, 1991–1993," *Slavic Review* 53, no. 2 (Summer 1994): 502.

7. See Edward N. Muller and Mitchell A. Seligson, "Civic Culture and Democracy: The Question of Causal Relationships," *The American Political Science Review* 88, no. 3 (September 1994): 635–652.

8. Aleksandr Kuranov, writing *Nezavisimaya Gazeta* (Moscow), reprinted in *World Press Review* (August 1994), p. 31.

9. To the best of my knowledge, J. Roland Pennock coined the term *political goods* in his article "Political Development, Political Systems, and Political Goods," *World Politics* 18, no. 2 (April 1966).

10. For accounts of these efforts, one might examine financier George Soros' *Underwriting Democracy* (New York: Free Press, 1991) or the National Democratic Institute's volume *New Democratic Frontier* (Washington, D.C.: NDI, 1992).

11. These assessments were reported in "Lessons of Western Technical Aid to Central and Eastern Europe: Beneficiaries Should Actively Participate," *Transition* (a bimonthly newsletter of the World Bank) 5, no. 6 (July–August 1994): 15.

12. See the U.S. Agency for International Development, Bureau for Europe and New Independent States, "Democracy Network Program," Request for Applications, No. ##-94–A-001 (issued June 15, 1994).

Selected Readings

Ambrose, Stephen E. *Rise to Globalism: American Foreign Policy Since 1938*, 6th rev. ed. New York: Penguin Books, 1991.

Ash, Timothy Garton. *In Europe's Name: Germany and the Divided Continent*. New York: Random House, 1993.

Bergner, Jeffrey T. *The New Superpower: Germany, Japan and the U.S. and the New World Order*. New York: St. Martin's Press, 1991.

Brzezinski, Zbigniew. *Out of Control: Global Turmoil on the Eve of the 21st Century*. New York: Charles Scribner's Sons, 1993.

Clark, Michael T., and Simon Serfaty, eds. *New Thinking and Old Realities: America, Europe, and Russia*. Washington, D.C.: Seven Locks Press, 1991.

Cleveland, Harland. *NATO: The Transatlantic Bargain*. New York: Harper and Row, 1970.

Deporte, Anton W. *Europe Between the Superpowers: The Enduring Balance*. New Haven, Conn.: Yale University Press, 1986.

Geipel, Gary. *Germany in a New Era*. Indianapolis: Hudson Institute, 1993.

Haftendorn, Helga, and Christian Tuschhoff, eds. *America and Europe in an Era of Change*. Boulder, Colo.: Westview Press, 1993.

Haass, Richard H. *Conflicts Unending: The United States and Regional Disputes*. New Haven, Conn.: Yale University Press, 1990.

Hewett, Ed A., and Victor H. Windays. *Milestones in Glasnost and Perestroyka: Politics and People*. Washington, D.C.: Brookings Institution, 1991.

——— . *Milestones in Glasnost and Perestroyka: The Economy*. Washington, D.C.: Brookings Institution, 1991.

Hogan, Michael J., ed. *The End of the Cold War: Its Meaning and Implications.* New York: Cambridge University Press, 1992.

Holborn, Hajo. *The Political Collapse of Europe.* New York: Alfred A. Knopf, 1951.

Huntington, Samuel. *The Third Wave: Democratization in the Late Twentieth Century.* Norman: University of Oklahoma Press, 1991.

Karp, Regina. *Central and Eastern Europe—The Challenges of Transition.* SIPRI. Oxford: Oxford University Press, 1993.

———, ed. *Security Without Nuclear Weapons? Different Perspectives on Non-Nuclear Security.* Oxford: Oxford University Press, 1992.

Kupcan, C., and C. Kupcan. "Concerts, Collective Security and the Future of Europe." *International Security* 16, no. 1 (Summer 1991): 114–161.

Jervis, Robert. *Perception and Misperception in International Politics.* Princeton, N.J.: Princeton University Press, 1976.

London, Kurt. *Eastern Europe in Transition.* Baltimore: Johns Hopkins University Press, 1966.

McCarthy, Patrick. *France-Germany, 1983–1993: The Struggle to Cooperate.* New York: St. Martin's Press, 1993.

McCauley, Martin, and Stephen Carter. *Leadership and Succession in the Soviet Union, Eastern Europe and China.* London: Macmillan, 1986.

Malloy, James M., and Mitchell Seligson, eds. *Democratic Transitions in Latin America.* Pittsburgh: University of Pittsburgh Press, 1987.

Nelson, Daniel N. *Alliance Behavior in the Warsaw Pact.* Boulder, Colo.: Westview Press 1986.

———. *The Balkan Imbroglio.* Boulder, Colo.: Westview Press, 1991.

———, and John Lampe. *East European Security Reconsidered.* Washington, D.C.: Johns Hopkins Univeristy Press, 1993.

Nye, Joseph S., ed. *International Regionalism.* Boston: Little, Brown and Company, 1968.

Plock, Ernest D. *East German-West German Relations and the Fall of the GDR.* Boulder, Colo.: Westview Press, 1993.

Rabe, Stephen. *Eisenhower and Latin America: The Foreign Policy of Anti-Communism.* Chapel Hill: Univeristy of North Carolina Press, 1988.

Rodman, Peter W. *More Precious Than Peace: The Cold War and the Struggle for the Third World.* New York: Charles Scribner's Sons, 1994.

Serfaty, Simon. *After Reagan: False Starts, Missed Opportunities and New Beginnings.* Washington, D.C.: Johns Hopkins University Press, 1988.

———. *American Foreign Policy in a Hostile World: Dangerous Years.* New York: Praeger, 1984.

———. *Taking Europe Seriously.* New York: St. Martin's Press, 1992.

Sloan, Stanley R. *NATO's Future.* Washington, D.C.: National Defense University Press, 1985.

Tiersky, Ronald. *France in the New Europe: Changing Yet Steadfast*. Belmont, Calif.: Wadsworth, 1994.

Treverton, Gregory F. *America, Germany and the Future of Europe*. Princeton, N.J.: Princeton University Press, 1992.

Vanhanen, Tatu. *The Process of Democratization: A Comparative Study of 147 States, 1980–88*. New York: Crane Russak, 1990.

White, Stephen. *Handbook of Reconstruction in Eastern Europe and the Soviet Union*. London: Longmans, 1991.

Index

Afghanistan, 121
AID (Agency for International Development), 170
Albania, 121
Alfonsín, Raúl, 7, 16
Argentina, 8; debt crisis, 20; the "disappeared," 28 n.3; economic gap between rich and poor, 27; economic recovery in 1980s, 21; human rights, 22–26; Mercosur, 22; military rebellion in 1987, 25; military rule, 19; military trials 23–25; obstacles to democratization, 19–21. *See also* Alfonsín, Raúl; Democratization
ARRC (Allied Command Europe Rapid Reaction Corps), 140
ASEAN (Association of Southeast Asian Nations), 132
Authoritarianism, 15–16, 87, 90; and modernization, 18. *See also* China, People's Republic of; De-

mocracy; Democratization; Eastern Europe

Balkans, 121; potential for instability, 95; and Russia, 123. *See also* Bosnia; Serbia; UN
Baltic States: independence movements, 44; and Russia, 115
Belgium, 5; ethnically mixed state, 127–28; and Zaïre, 79
Bolivia, 2
Bosnia, 158; ethnic minorities, 127; failure of West, 105; and the UN, 124–25. *See also* Balkans; Ethnic conflict; NATO; Serbia; UN
Boutros-Ghali, Boutros, 122
Brazil, 8
Bulgaria, 44–46; environmentalism, 55; public attitudes toward regime, 47–49, 54–55. *See also* Eastern Europe; Warsaw Pact
Bush, George, 119, 160

Contributors

RAÚL ALFONSÍN, former president of Argentina, risked his life re-creating a democracy after the war in the Malvinas/Falkland Islands. He was president of Argentina from 1983 to 1989, when, for the first time in several years, the presidency was passed on through the democratic process. During his time in office, Alfonsín initiated negotiations that achieved peace with Argentina's neighbor Chile. President Alfonsín also created CONADEP (National Commission of Disappeared Persons), which he summarized in a book published around the world, *Never Again*. This volume led to the trial and conviction of leaders of the military Junta. His most notable achievements include the implementation of the National Plan for Literacy, recognized by UNESCO (United Nations Educational, Scientific and Cultural Organizations) and PAN (National Plan for Nutrition), which has served as a model of social change for other Latin American countries.

FLORIBERT CHEBEYA is president of Voice of the Voiceless, a human rights organization in Zaïre, and is one of the country's most important human rights activists. His organization advocates the transition toward a multiparty democratic government. In 1992, he received the prestigious "Reebok Human Rights Award."

ROBERT A. DAHL, the world's principal theorist on democracy, is a Sterling Professor of Political Science and professor emeritus at Yale

University. Dahl received his Ph.D. from Yale in 1940 and has taught at the university since 1946. He is the author of eighteen books, the most recent being the widely acclaimed *Democracy and Its Critics*, plus numerous articles.

REGINA KARP is an associate professor in Old Dominion University's Graduate Programs in International Studies. Karp has served as senior researcher and project leader at the Stockholm International Peace Research Institute (SIPRI) since 1987. Before joining SIPRI she was a resident fellow at the Institute for East-West Security Studies in New York and a postdoctoral fellow at the Center for Arms Control and International Security at Stanford University.

LIU BINYAN is a visiting scholar at Princeton University in the China Initiative Program. He is the publisher of *China Watch*, a publication of the Princeton China Initiative. He has published works in both the United States and China. During World War II, Dr. Liu organized anti-Japanese underground activities. Since the communist takeover in China, Liu's criticisms of government policy have led to severe punishments—twice he was banished to agricultural "reform through labor" programs and twice expelled from the party. He received an honorary doctorate of letters from Trinity College in 1990.

CHARLES WILLIAM MAYNES, editor of *Foreign Policy* since 1980, is a 1960 graduate of Harvard University. Maynes began work for the Carnegie Endowment for International Peace in 1972 as director of its International Organization Program. Maynes was named assistant secretary of state for international peace in 1977 by the Carter administration, in which capacity he was responsible for U.S. policy at the United Nations and its specialized agencies.

PAUL DAVID MILLER Admiral, U.S. Navy (Ret.) President of Sperry Marine, Inc. Previously, he was the Supreme Allied Commander in the Atlantic. In addition to duties with the Navy Staff (Strategic Plans Division), Admiral Miller served as deputy chief of naval operations and as commander in chief, United States Atlantic Fleet. He earned a master's degree from the University of Georgia. Admiral Miller is also a graduate of the Naval War College and the Harvard Business Executive Management Program.

DANIEL N. NELSON is director of the Graduate Programs in International Studies at Old Dominion University in Norfolk, Virginia. Previously, he served as the senior foreign and defense policy advisor for the majority leader of the U.S. House of Representatives, Representative Richard Gephardt, and was a foreign policy consultant in Senator Tom Harkin's presidential campaign. In 1990, he was a senior associate at the Carnegie Endowment writing on Eastern Europe and European security, and (from 1977 to 1989) a professor of political science at the University of Kentucky.

SIMON SERFATY is a professor at Old Dominion University's Graduate Programs in International Studies. Serfaty currently serves as a research professor of U.S. foreign policy at the Johns Hopkins School of Advanced International Studies (SAIS). He also has held the positions of director of the SAIS Center of European Studies in Bologna, Italy, director of the Washington Center of Foreign Policy Research, and most recently, executive director of the Johns Hopkins Foreign Policy Institute. Serfaty also worked as associate editor for Western Europe with Business International in New York. A recipient of the New School's Albert Camus Prize in New York, Serfaty taught courses in U.S. foreign policy and European studies at the University of California at Los Angeles.

ISBN 0-313-29393-7

90000>

EAN

9 780313 293931